How to Get Your Message Out Fast & Free Using Podcasts

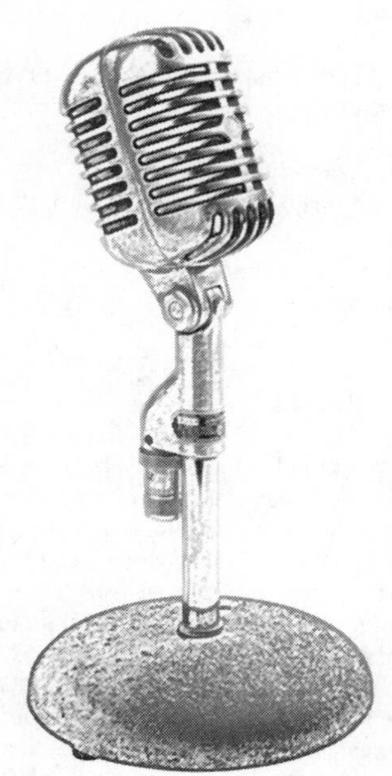

Everything You Need to Know About Podcasting Explained Simply

By Kevin Walker

How to Get Your Message Out Fast & Free Using Podcasts: Everything You Need to Know About Podcasting Explained Simply

1405 SW 6th Avenue • Ocala, Florida 34471 • Phone 800-814-1132 • Fax 352-622-1875
Web site: www.atlantic-pub.com • E-mail: sales@atlantic-pub.com
SAN Number: 268-1250

Walker, Kevin, 1981-
How to get your message out fast & free using podcasts : everything you need to know about podcasting explained simply / by Kevin Walker.
p. cm.
Includes bibliographical references and index.
ISBN-13: 978-1-60138-120-0 (alk. paper)
ISBN-10: 1-60138-120-4 (alk. paper)
1. Podcasting. 2. Webcasting. 3. Internet marketing. I. Title. II. Title: How to get your message out fast and free using podcasts.
TK5105.887.W36 2010
659.20285'67876--dc22
2010043095

Printed in the United States

PROJECT MANAGER: Melissa Peterson • mpeterson@atlantic-pub.com
INTERIOR DESIGN: Jackie Miller • millerjackiej@gmail.com
PROOFREADER: Brett Daly • brett.daly1@gmail.com
FRONT & BACK COVER DESIGNS: Jackie Miller • millerjackiej@gmail.com

Printed on Recycled Paper

We recently lost our beloved pet "Bear," who was not only our best and dearest friend but also the "Vice President of Sunshine" here at Atlantic Publishing. He did not receive a salary but worked tirelessly 24 hours a day to please his parents. Bear was a rescue dog that turned around and showered myself, my wife Sherri, his grandparents Jean, Bob and Nancy and every person and animal he met (maybe not rabbits) with friendship and love. He made a lot of people smile every day.

We wanted you to know that a portion of the profits of this book will be donated to The Humane Society of the United States. *–Douglas & Sherri Brown*

The human-animal bond is as old as human history. We cherish our animal companions for their unconditional affection and acceptance. We feel a thrill when we glimpse wild creatures in their natural habitat or in our own backyard.

Unfortunately, the human-animal bond has at times been weakened. Humans have exploited some animal species to the point of extinction.

The Humane Society of the United States makes a difference in the lives of animals here at home and worldwide. The HSUS is dedicated to creating a world where our relationship with animals is guided by compassion. We seek a truly humane society in which animals are respected for their intrinsic value, and where the human-animal bond is strong.

Want to help animals? We have plenty of suggestions. Adopt a pet from a local shelter, join The Humane Society and be a part of our work to help companion animals and wildlife. You will be funding our educational, legislative, investigative and outreach projects in the U.S. and across the globe.

Or perhaps you'd like to make a memorial donation in honor of a pet, friend or relative? You can through our Kindred Spirits program. And if you'd like to contribute in a more structured way, our Planned Giving Office has suggestions about estate planning, annuities, and even gifts of stock that avoid capital gains taxes.

Maybe you have land that you would like to preserve as a lasting habitat for wildlife. Our Wildlife Land Trust can help you. Perhaps the land you want to share is a backyard—that's enough. Our Urban Wildlife Sanctuary Program will show you how to create a habitat for your wild neighbors.

So you see, it's easy to help animals. And The HSUS is here to help.

2100 L Street NW • Washington, DC 20037 • 202-452-1100
www.hsus.org

Dedication

To my wife Amber.

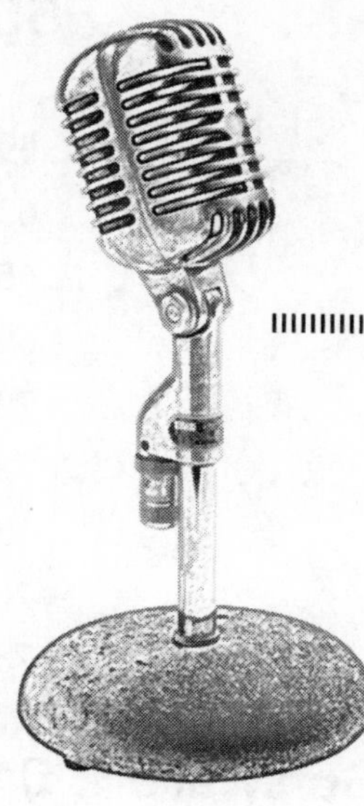

Table of Contents

Introduction

Welcome to the world of podcasting. You are about to embark on a rewarding and fulfilling new endeavor that has already excited thousands of others just like you, from professional broadcasters to teenagers in basements.

You might be like Steven Winters. Winters has always harbored the desire to be a DJ or host his own talk show like David Letterman or Jerry Springer. However, no television studios or radio stations were forthcoming with a contract, so he turned to podcasting. Once a week, Winters pulls out his own microphone and provides anecdotes and stories for an audience of thousands with his show, *Up Late with Steven Winters*.

Or, perhaps you are like Patricia Hunt, a small business owner and independent software developer who wanted a better way to promote her products than expensive online and print advertisements. Podcasting was the answer. For a fraction of the cost of a traditional advertising campaign, Hunt started her own podcast on a subject she knew her potential clients would be interested in. And, if she candidly suggests that her own software is a solution to a problem, she would not be the first small business owner to discover that a few hours with a microphone and a few dollars in hosting fees saves her thousands in marketing expenses.

You could also be just like me a few years ago; you could have a passion you want to share with the world. I wanted to share my enthusiasm for the writings of an obscure, early 20th century English essayist named Gilbert Keith Chesterton. Because he is long dead and his work is in the public domain, I began recording audio books of many of his most popular essays. I did not promote a product or entertain thousands with my own wit. I simply shared a passion and have since met thousands who share that passion – some of whom discovered the obscure "Prince of Paradox" entirely through my own efforts.

Or, maybe you are just curious.

Whatever your reason for being interested in podcasting, you have taken your first step toward entering the world of Internet multimedia and getting your message out there.

What is Podcasting?

Podcasting is an Internet technology that allows an individual or business to self-publish multimedia content to the computers and portable media players of his or her audience directly and automatically. Perhaps the easiest way to describe podcasting is sion is another great success, and it even addresses one of the weaknesses of radio: It is not limited to just sound. Full-motion video is broadcast on most channels, and now, many channels even offer their video in high-definition. A third of households are estimated have a high-definition television, according to the Nielsen Company, and that number is growing rapidly.

Aside from video, however, television possesses the same flaws as radio. Setting up a television station is even more expensive than setting up an FM radio station. Because there are only so many frequencies available for television to broadcast on, nature puts the same limits on how many over-the-air television stations can broadcast at a one time in a given city, and the efforts of the FCC to ration the frequencies into licenses make a television frequency in an urban area worth millions of dollars.

There has to be a better way.

Podcasting

Enter podcasting. Podcasting is the only technology that addresses all the disadvantages of radio and television. Though most podcasts are audio-only, video podcasts, also sometimes called vodcasts, are growing in popularity, and many publishers choose to offer both audio and video versions of their content. Some podcasts even publish high-definition video.

Podcasting is also inexpensive. Even the most professionally produced podcasts only require approximately $5,000 to get started, but assuming you already have a personal computer and a quiet room in your home, you can get a respectable podcast on the Internet for less than the price of a nice meal at a restaurant.

Because there are no frequencies to divvy up, there are no licensing requirements or limits to the number of podcasts available at any given time. There are roughly 9,725 licensed FM radio stations in the United States, and only 100 of them are available in any one city. TV cable providers boast that they provide around 200 channels of content. By mid-2007, there were 125,000 podcasts in existence with a total audience of around 60 million people.

Podcasting is growing every day. Unlike radio and local television, your potential audience is not limited to the people that live in your area. Instead, your potential audience includes every person on Earth who uses the Internet, speaks your language, and is interested in your topic. For example, there are 1.5 billion people on Earth who speak English, either as a native or second language, and about 500 million of them use the Internet.

Even topics of incredibly narrow interest can have a large enough audience to inspire jealousy in some of the more traditional forms of media. I have a friend who is an editor for a general interest newspaper for a suburb of a major American city. His paper reaches 10,000 readers a week. Successful podcasts regularly bring in a larger audience because podcasting fishes in a larger pool. An example would be Rhonda Rivera's *Ear on Careers* podcast, which regularly brings in over 50,000 listeners.

CASE STUDY: BIG MEDIA SIZE AUDIENCES

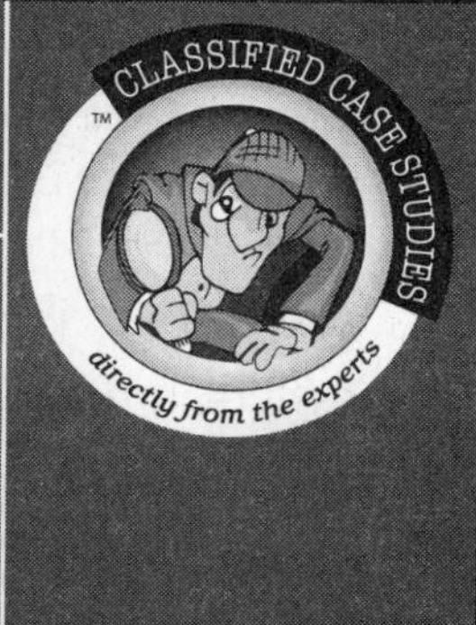

Rhonda Rivera, co-founder
Ear On Careers
Top-Tier Tutoring, LLC
623 Eagle Rock Avenue
#204, West Orange, NJ 07052
Phone: (973) 243-1212
Fax: (973) 243-1213
www.top-tiertutoring.com
www.earoncareers.com
rhonda@top-tiertutoring.com

Rhonda Rivera is the co-founder of Top-Tier Tutoring, a college counseling and tutoring center for university-bound high school students. She started *Ear on Careers* as a way to let students know about growing careers and hear interviews from professionals in different fields so that they can make informed choices about their universities and majors. Her favorite part of the show is looking for her guests — professionals in a wide-range of careers, from academia to business and industry.

Her advice for dealing with guests is to always let the guest see all the questions in advance so they can prepare, along with an information sheet about the show and what they can expect. In particular, she suggests that podcasters let guests know that mistakes can be easily removed later as a way to help them relax.

Ear on Careers has been running since mid-2009, and Rhonda says she spends around five hours preparing for each 20-minute episode of her show. The biggest problem she sees in many podcasts is poor audio quality and inconsistency. Her advice for new podcasters: Just try it. As long as you produce good, evergreen content, people will want to hear what you have to say.

Finally, podcasting is not live. Though you can have a show available to your listeners within minutes of hitting the record button, podcasting is designed to be enjoyed at the listener's leisure. Once listeners discover your podcast, all they need to do is click the "subscribe" button to ensure that they always have your freshest content available to play any time.

Earlier, I described podcasting as an Internet technology, but it is more accurate to say that podcast technology actually depends on an entire network of Internet technologies, most of which were not created with podcasting in mind.

RSS feeds

The key technology that stands behind the publishing side of podcasting is the RSS feed. RSS stands for Really Simple Syndication, and aside from some of the technical details, it really is a simple process to understand. RSS feeds allow people to subscribe to their favorite news sources, blogs, and podcasts and let their computers automatically collect new additions in one place on their computer: a program called an aggregator — or, in the case of podcasts, a podcatcher. Even though podcasting exceeds the simple text and pictures that the creators of RSS feeds had in mind when creating the technology, the two are an excellent fit.

An RSS feed functions like a table of contents that can be easily updated. When a new episode is added to a podcast, the table of contents is updated to reflect the new entry. When the aggregator/podcatcher checks the table of contents, which it does regularly throughout the day, it sees the new episodes listed and downloads them. In fact, an RSS feed is really just a single text file written in a special computer language called XML, or Extensible Markup Language.

Do not panic.

You will probably never need to deal with the XML of your podcast's RSS feed by hand. Many free tools exist to automate the process of updating the feed whenever new content goes live. However, it is important to have at least a basic understanding of how the RSS feed works in order to be prepared to deal with problems. *Chapter 8 will cover RSS feeds in greater detail.*

Podcast directories and podcatchers

Potential listeners will usually find your podcast by browsing through a podcast directory for topics that interest them. The podcast directory simply keeps a list of all the RSS feeds and gives users an easy way to browse and search for podcasts. The most popular podcast directory is the one hosted by Apple in the iTunes® Store, but there are others such as Podcast Alley and National Public Radio's Podcast Directory. There are even podcast directories that only host specific types of podcasts. For example, if you have a Christian podcast, you might want to look at Godcast 1000, a directory for Christian podcasters. In order to have a successful podcast, you should submit your show to as many directories as possible. ITunes might be No. 1, but being listed in podcast directories is free, and you do not want to lose listeners just because they prefer a podcast directory you are not in. *This will be described in greater detail in Chapter 9.*

When listeners find podcasts they are interested in, they click a subscribe link in that directory to add it to the list of their subscriptions. The subscription list is managed by a program on the listener's computer called a podcatcher. If RSS feeds are the heart of podcasting for the publisher, podcatchers are the heart for listeners. After a user subscribes to a podcast, these programs leap into action. For as long as the computer is turned on and the podcatcher is running, it will automatically check the RSS feed for that podcast every few minutes to see if any new episodes have become available. If new episodes are available, the podcatcher starts downloading them automatically. As long as the listener has his or her computer turned on and the podcatcher program running, new episodes will be downloaded and ready to play as soon as they are released. If the listener turns the computer off for a few hours, days, or weeks, as soon as the podcatcher is turned back on, it will check the RSS feed for all the subscribed podcasts, discover all the missed episodes, and faithfully download them.

Many podcatchers, such as the iTunes application produced by Apple to work with its iPod® MP3 players, will even move new episodes onto an MP3 player automatically as soon as it is connected to the computer. This ensures that your audience always has the latest episodes, even on the road.

Some Popular Podcatchers

Apple iTunes: The king of the hill. ITunes is so popular that you can design your podcasts just for this program. If your podcast works in iTunes, then it should work in all other programs. However, because iTunes is so popular, it has given Apple the power to give you headaches in a few other ways. *See Chapter 8 on RSS feeds for more information.*

Amarok: Amarok is a popular iTunes-alternative for Linux users, though some Windows users use it also.

Podcast.com: Podcast.com is a twist on the traditional podcatcher software. With Podcast.com, users only subscribe to the podcasts. They are never downloaded to the listener's computer until the last possible moment, as a stream. In this sense, it is less like iTunes and more like the popular YouTube video service.

Media Monkey: Media Monkey is another iTunes replacement for Windows users.

Some Popular Podcast Directories

Apple iTunes: This is the most popular directory. Unless you are intent on distributing content that iTunes does not allow, you want to make sure you have an entry in the Apple iTunes directory. You should also make sure your podcast uses all the features available on iTunes.

Podcast Alley: Podcast Alley adds a greater social dimension for podcast creators and listeners. In addition to the standard directory searching features, there is a community forum, blog, and regularly updated featured podcast list. It is also one of the largest podcast directories outside the iTunes directory, with over 86,000 podcasts.

National Public Radio Podcast Directory: The National Public Radio (NPR) Podcast Directory, unlike most other podcast directories, is not open for new podcasts. Instead, it provides a central repository for podcasts being published by brick and mortar radio stations around the country.

What You Should Learn From This Book

The goal is of this book is simple. You will learn what podcasting is, what it can do for you, and what listeners will expect of you when you begin your own podcast. You will discover the tricks and tips necessary to create a high-quality podcast that will draw an audience of listeners and/or viewers without breaking the bank.

You will also learn how to market and brand your podcast to gain listeners as quickly as possible, because no one wants to go through the work of creating a podcast and find themselves speaking into the void of the Internet. You will learn the most common strategies professional podcasters use to monetize their podcast and turn their passion into a career.

Although this book is not intended to be a computer science textbook, you should also gain a grasp of the technical side of podcasting. This will allow you to make informed decisions about the plethora of hosting services and software available for potential podcasters and avoid some unnecessary expenses often placed on unsuspecting and technologically un-savvy podcasters. You will also be able to effectively deal with the rapid changes that constantly occur in the computer industry. A little technical knowledge will prevent you from making mistakes such as committing your podcasts to a dying technology.

Finally, this book will give you a basic understanding of some of the legal issues that are important in podcasting today. Though I am not a lawyer and cannot offer legal advice for your specific situation, at the end of this book, you should have a clear vision of the principles that govern your rights of intellectual property (IP), how to protect your own IP, and how to work with the IP of others without receiving cease-and-desist letters in the mail. It is very fashionable today to take a cavalier attitude toward the IP rights of others, but one thing is certain: Settling your IP rights and licenses ahead of time is a lot cheaper and easier than settling them in court.

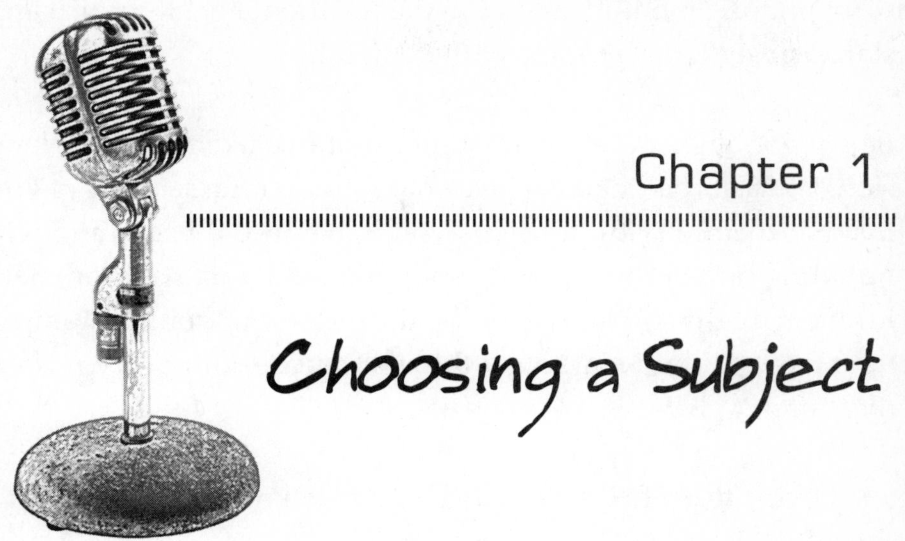

Chapter 1

Choosing a Subject

You cannot have a podcast without a subject, and no matter how wrapped up in mysterious jargon and technical details podcasting might seem, the subject matter is the most important part of your podcast. If you have a great subject, your listeners might even forgive some background noise or minor quality issues that affect the rest of your podcast. If you have a poor subject, not even a million-dollar sound studio will save it. This is not TV or radio: Your listeners have hundreds of thousands of podcasts from which to choose.

In all likelihood, you already have a subject in mind. Actually, saying you have a subject in mind might be an understatement. When children get their hands on a dollar, their mothers would say it was burning a hole in their pocket, as they instantly rushed to the store to spend it. If you have an interest in starting a podcast, then your idea is likely burning a hole in your head. You want nothing more than to grab the microphone, hit record, and start sharing your message with the world.

Be patient. Remember, podcasting is not live like radio or television. Podcasts do not disappear into space within seconds of you making them. Hasty decisions you make in the beginning will be sitting on your server, plaguing you for years. Later on, new listeners might still judge you by the content of your first impatient release. You want to get the first release, and every release thereafter, right.

So, the first thing to do, even if you already know your topic, is to ask yourself two big questions:

- What is the goal?
- What niche does it fill?

What is the Goal?

Another way of putting this is: What is in it for you? Podcasting is work, especially if you want to do a decent job of it, so you must understand why you are going to put forth all this effort. If you are looking for a get-rich-quick scheme or even just a hobby you can use to fill five or ten spare minutes a week, you are getting into the wrong thing.

Each hour of broadcasted material is generally the product of three to four hours of writing, recording, and post-production spent editing out mistakes, such as stutters or unnaturally long pauses, which are known as dead air. Compared to traditional media like radio and television, this is not much, but it is a fair

amount of work for one person. The people that work in traditional media have thought long and hard about what they want, so should you.

There are three broad reasons someone would start his or her own podcast:

- To spread the word about a topic
- To share a passion
- To promote something or someone

Spreading the word

Most people have a strong opinion on at least one issue. They want to bring the world around to their way of thinking and, hopefully, make the world a better place by doing so. For example, an environmentalist might see podcasting as a new way to encourage people to show Mother Earth a little tender loving care. You might have a few choice words for or against a certain political leader or party. You might think the traditional media outlets do a poor job of covering some issues and want to take on the role of media watchdog.

Whatever the case, you are not alone, and from its beginnings in the early 2000s, podcasting has been a way to get the word out about a topic and give ordinary people a chance to say what they think needs to be said. This is the goal of Lillian Brummet, a woman out to change the world for the better with her *Conscious Discussions* podcast. Every other Sunday, she invites guests to speak to thousands of listeners around the world and take questions from the live chat room. The topics range from environmentalism to how to help the poor, and guests call in from as far away as Africa and Europe.

CASE STUDY: OUT TO CHANGE THE WORLD

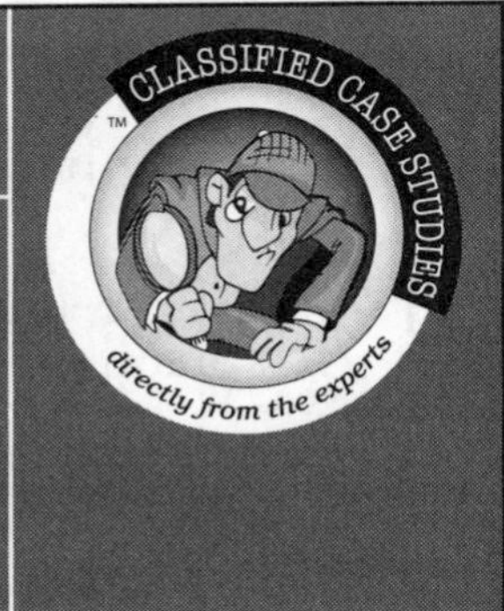

Lillian Brummet, host and author
Conscious Discussions
PO Box 747, Grand Forks,
British Columbia, Canada, VOH 1HO
www.blogtalkradio.com/
consciousdiscussions
ldbrummet@gmail.com

Every other Sunday, Lillian Brummet uploads an episode of *Conscious Discussions*, an hour-long talk show designed to celebrate people from around the world trying to make the world a better place. Guests from around the world are interviewed, with some calling in from as far away as Africa, Australia, and Europe, and she boasts a listenership of over 50,000. She is also the author of two books: *Trash Talk: An inspirational guide to saving time and money through better waste and resource management* and *Purple Snowflake Marketing: How to Make Your Book Stand Out in a Crowd*, which discusses self-publishing.

One feature Brummet uses to stand out from the crowd is her live chat room. She uses BlogTalkRadio to broadcast her shows using live streaming technology. She invites guests to visit the chat room and talk about the show and fields the best questions asked in the chat room by her guests. She says that, on average, it takes her about five hours of preparation time before her one-hour episodes are ready to go live.

Her advice for new podcasters: Stay organized, research your guests, and let your audience give you inspiration. As for monetization, *Conscious Discussions* has periodic advertisements, but they only bring in pennies per episode. However, the chance to network with her listeners and let listeners know about her published books and other services makes it all worthwhile.

Another example is Nancy Brown. She is the host of *UnCommon Sense*, the official podcast of the American Chesterton Society, and the purpose of the podcast, like the society that pays its bills, is to tell people about what they consider simultaneously both the greatest and most neglected writer of the 20th century, his diagnosis of the world's ills, and his solutions.

CASE STUDY: SPREADING THE WORD

Nancy Brown, podcast head
UnCommon Sense
The American Chesterton Society
4117 Pebblebrook Circle,
Minneapolis, MN 5543
http://uncommonsense.libsyn.com
info@chesterton.org
Phone: (952) 831-3096
Fax: (852) 831-0387

The American Chesterton Society
4117 Pebblebrook Circle
Minneapolis, MN 55437

The *Uncommon Sense* podcast is the official podcast of the American Chesterton Society, an association dedicated to fostering appreciation of the British essayist and novelist, G.K. Chesterton. Chesterton was a prolific writer at the turn of the century, writing almost constantly until his death in 1936. He published everything from children's poetry and detective stories to newspaper articles and anti-Nazi polemics.

The American Chesterton Society is a largely volunteer-based organization, which describes Nancy Brown's role as the head of the *UnCommon Sense* podcast — she volunteered for it. For her, it is a labor of love. She wants people to know who Chesterton was and why people like her believe books and newspaper articles written a hundred years ago are still relevant today.

She records the podcast on a Mac laptop with the GarageBand software described in this book and uses a USB dynamic microphone. If listeners complain about sound quality, she just invites them to make a donation to support her fund for a better mic. Episodes are released roughly every two weeks, and her marketing strategy was simple: Chesterton already has an existing fan base, so she just sought to let them know the podcast existed. Her advice for new podcasters: "My first podcasts were less than stellar, but I've improved [because] I was brave enough to do it before I knew what I was doing. Don't be afraid. Just start."

Sharing your passion

Maybe you have a passion, but you do not really have an agenda. Maybe you just want to share the excitement of chess, Japanese robot movies, astronomy, or German board games with as many people as possible. Chances are, if you are passionate about something, whether it is mainstream or obscure, you will have an audience of like-minded people — and an even larger audience of curious onlookers.

This is probably the most common motivation for amateur podcasters. It can be exhilarating to share a personal passion and become part of a network of thousands of people who feel the same way.

One podcaster who uses his show as a way to share his passion is Corey Coehler, host of *Musicgoat Melting Pot*. Koehler is a musician who loves music and wants to share his favorites with as many people as he can. So, whenever the urge takes him, he fires up the microphone, talks a bit about a favorite song, and gives a performance for his listeners.

A few more podcasters out to share their passion are Chad Fifer and Chris Lackey, who have loved the fiction of horror writer H.P. Lovecraft since the days of their youth. Fifer even boasts that, as a teenager, he was a member in a Lovecraft-themed garage band. They have no agenda; they like Lovecraft and want more people to enjoy him. Nor do they take their favorite writer too seriously: They first had the idea while mocking their own animated film, based on a Lovecraft story.

CASE STUDY: A LIFELONG PASSION

Chad Fifer, creator and host
Chris Lackey, creator and host
H.P. Lovecraft Literary Podcast
www.hppodcraft.com
chadfifer@yahoo.com

Chad Fifer and Chris Lackey have been fans of horror writer H.P. Lovecraft since they were growing up together. They played the *Call of Cthulhu* game, they have done movie adaptions of Lovecraft stories, and Chad Fifer even had a Lovecraft inspired garage band. After working on the *Call of Cthulhu* movie released in 2005, the pair chose to start a podcast during a lull in their movie and television projects. The final decision came while they were recording a DVD commentary track making fun of their own animated Lovecraft film, *The Chosen One.*

Of all the aspects of the show, they say the recording is the best part. They share little of their pre-episode prep-work with one another before the show, believing that the conversation will sound more natural if they are sincerely reacting to one another's ideas. However, they warn not to steam roll your co-host. If one host seems to overwhelm the other on a particular episode, they suggest editing out sections in post-production to ensure that shows have a balanced feel. Chad Fifer says the most common mistake he sees in other podcasters is that they will often forget their own listeners. "Hosts are only a part of the show, and the listener is the more important part. I've turned quite a few podcasts off because of the hosts' rambling about unrelated topics or overusing inside jokes."

Promotional podcasting

Finally, you might have something or someone you want to promote. Though a great many people start their podcast to share some passion or argue for some point of view, there are some prominent examples of promotional podcasts out there. Podcasting can be a great tool to drum up excitement about a new product or service just coming on the market. There is one great caveat to promotional podcasting, however: You still have to deliver a podcast people want to listen to. You will not have legions of fans adding a series of commercials to their iPods. It is going to take some creativity to find a topic that interests your listeners, but allows you to engage in your promotion at the same time, but it has been done before.

Many traditional newspapers and magazines, such as *The Economist*, are putting out limited podcasts in order to entice subscribers to their papers and magazines, allowing people to receive more stories in greater detail. Every week, they publish the "Editor's highlights," a selection of editorials and in-depth news stories from the print magazine, along with a plug for the print version should listeners wish to know more.

Manga Entertainment, a translator and publisher of Japanese comic books and cartoons in the United States, takes another route. Every few weeks it releases a free Japanese comic book and animation podcast called *Manga Minutes*. In addition to reviews, *Manga Minutes* talks about things of interest for its fans, such as upcoming conventions and interviews with important people in that industry. And as you can imagine, Manga's own products fare pretty well in the reviews.

Magnatune takes another, yet more daring, approach. This independent music label has a collection of dozens of podcasts for different music genres (ranging from heavy metal to neo-Renaissance) and rotates through the singles in its catalog through a series of hour-long podcasts. The strategy is simple: People come to Magnatune for the free music, discover a new artist, and either buy the full album or pay a monthly subscription fee to get access to the whole catalog without the nagging messages at the beginning and end of each free podcast episode.

These are three examples of successful promotional podcasts that succeed in giving their audiences what they want while promoting their products and not making their listeners feel like they are sitting through commercials.

CASE STUDY: AN IMOVIE-BASED PODCAST

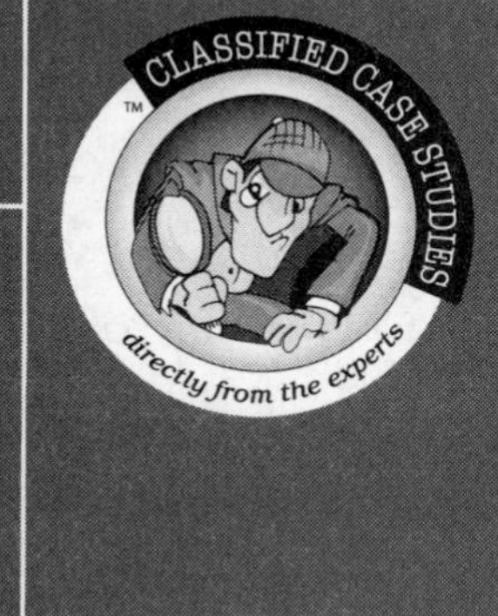

Chaz Rough, founder
YOGAmazing
211 Clover Lane
Louisville, Kentuky 40207
Phone: (502) 896-9642
www.yogamazing.com
chaz@yogamazing.com

Chaz Rough produces the *YOGAmazing* video podcast from his Yoga training studio in Louisville, Kentuky. He started the show with a humble 15-frame-per-second Kodak digital camera and did the editing in iMovie with the goal of promoting his yoga instruction business and at the prompting of his students. That was five years ago. His videos have since been downloaded over twelve million times, and he has upgraded to a Canon XH-A1 digital camcorder and uses Final Cut Pro for editing. His videos have been sponsored by everyone from Coca-Cola to Zone Perfect Health Bars, and he sells old instructional videos for $1.99 a piece. He has been featured in Yoga Journal, Shape Magazine, and Parenting Magazine, and his instructional videos have been rated some of the best in the iTunes directory in 2008 and 2009. But his favorite part is the interaction it gives him with a wider community of people who share his interests. His advice for new podcasters: "Be yourself [and] always launch on the same day at the same time so people know when to expect the content."

What Niche Does It Fill?

If you already have a topic, hopefully this question is pretty easy to answer, but you still need to explicitly answer this question. The more refined your answer, the better.

Narrowcasting and the niche

In fact, the word "niche" here is being used for a reason. Whereas radio and television are examples of broadcasting, podcasting means narrowcasting: targeting your podcast to a narrow segment of the popular. As discussed in the Introduction of this book, one of the weaknesses of traditional multimedia is that it must target extremely broad demographics in order to be viable. By comparison, as a podcaster, your costs are low, and if you plan on podcasting in English, you audience pool is literally measured in the hundreds of millions. Sounds great, but your competition is in the hundreds of thousands. Your audience is looking for something that caters specifically to them. A broad topic will not be noticed. Board game fans are not looking for podcasts about "board games," but they are looking for "German board games" and "tabletop war games." A podcast about hiking will not get as

much attention as a podcast about "ultra light backpacking" or "hiking the Pacific Crest Trail."

Imagine one of your listeners: a bicycle lover in search of a bicycle podcast, for example. A search of the iTunes directory for podcasts about "bicycles" reveals hundreds of podcasts about bicycles, with more coming out every day. As an aspiring podcaster, you can either hang your head in despair at the odds of being noticed in a crowd of hundreds, or you can take advantage of an opportunity.

A podcast about "bicycles" might not be noticed; however, the imaginary listener is not just a bicycle lover. He or she is a cross-country cyclist who loves riding a bicycle to the lake to go camping. Out of the hundreds of "bicycle" podcasts in the iTunes directory, how many cater to him or her specifically? A quick search for "cross-country cycling" and "bicycle camping" at the time of publication resulted in three and only one or two others that mention the subject in passing. There is an opportunity to reach this listener, as well as the thousands of potential listeners who share this interest.

Broadcasting and posting generic information on a broad subject might work well for television and radio because there are only a few dozen stations from which to choose. How many television shows or radio programs have you seen that are dedicated to cross-country cycling? Podcasting is more intimate, and the key to standing out from the crowd is narrowcasting.

You can use two strategies to narrow your podcast's subject. Hyper-specialization has already been discussed: Instead of making your podcast about "cycling," you can make it about cross-country cycling, bicycle camping, or lightweight biking. This is by far the most common way podcasters find their niche. You can also try hyper-localization, which is producing a podcast for a narrowly defined geographic area. Instead of going from biking to cross-country biking, you might decide to devote a podcast to "biking in Chicago" or "biking in southwest Texas."

Who do you want your listeners to be?

Consider these two entries from a typical blog:

- "Today, I had a sandwich for lunch with Kim. Here's a photo."
- "Yesterday, I watched the first Star Wars with Joe. Good movie."

You can probably take a good guess as to who this person's audience is: a small circle of his or her relatives and acquaintances. For that matter, many bloggers write for an audience of one, and some podcasters seem to do that as well. There is nothing wrong with this; websites and blogs are free and plenty of people just want to let their friends, and only their friends, know what is on their minds. However, if you are contemplating a podcast, chances are you have a wider circle in mind than the people you already know. After all, there are easier ways to keep in touch with friends than a podcast.

So, who exactly is your audience? The answer is usually pretty obvious. If you are doing a podcast about end-game chess strategies, your audience might be other chess lovers or newcomers to the game. Or, it could be general gamers you want to entice into

chess. However, there are more subtle aspects to deciding what type of audience to target.

For example, suppose you decide to podcast about off-road bicycling, so your listeners are amateur cyclists, but no one person can be summed up with the phrase "amateur cyclist." Who is your audience really? You can probably make a few assumptions with a great deal of certainty. They are athletic. They are health conscious. You can probably make a few more by connecting the dots. Most of them are young to middle-aged adults. They might be more likely to care about environmental issues. You do not need to commission a study by the Nielsen Company to get this overview either. Do some research. If magazines or websites exist for your subject, take a look at what is being advertised. If there is a Web forum, take a look around the forums and see if you notice any patterns.

Form a picture of the audience you are targeting before you move on to the next question because this picture will influence your decisions about the podcast from here on out.

What will you give them?

Now that you know whom you want to tune in, you need to decide why they should tune in. This is not about free promotional giveaways, like T-shirts or books, though some podcasts decide to take that course. You need to know what will bring people to your show and deliver it.

If the show is about kitchen herb gardening, talk about that. This sounds obvious, but it is incredibly easy and surprisingly common to stray off topic when sitting in front of an open mic.

There is nothing wrong with talking about the latest amusing thing your cat has done, provided you are podcasting about pets. If your podcast is about German board games, conservative politics, or French food, however, your audience will quickly grow bored and stop listening. This can be especially difficult when a person's motive for podcasting is his or her own passion for a subject. It is easy to let another passion derail the theme of a show, especially if the new passion is more exciting at the moment.

If a person tunes into your podcast about bicycling across America, it means he or she wants to hear about cycling. Digressions are OK, but only if they lead back to the topic quickly. So, if your amusing cat anecdote somehow relates to your topic, go for it. Otherwise, leave it out completely.

Can you talk about this topic?

Podcasting is narrowcasting, and you need to find your niche. However, it is possible to take this too far. There very well might be a big enough audience to support a podcast about varieties of grass native to Northeast Texas, but the bigger question is whether you can keep a show going, week after week, month after month, year after year with interesting new things to say about native Texas grasses.

Ultimately, you are the sole arbiter of whether a topic is too narrow for you, but a few guiding principles will prevent you from committing yourself to an impossibly small task:

- **Go with what you are interested in.** If you have a topic you could talk about until your friends and family leave the room, congratulations. Someone out there feels the same way.
- **Brainstorm a few months' worth of shows.** If you can easily come up with topics for ten or 15 shows, you are probably in good shape. More will come as you produce the show, and you might find yourself constantly putting off a few of your original show ideas. However, if the first dozen topics do not come effortlessly and quickly, the topic might actually be too small of a niche.

Promotional Planning

You have your idea and are filled with passion and ready to get the word out. You have found your niche, and you know who your audience is. You even have a dozen or so ideas for which topics to cover in your first few months of episodes. Now what?

It is time to think about how people are going to find your podcast and hear your message. Podcast directories like iTunes and Podcast Alley allow users to search for you, but those users are usually not sitting in front of iTunes 24 hours a day running keyword searches. In order to get the word out effectively, you are going to need to be more proactive than waiting for your listeners to find you.

A word about spam

The first temptation many people face when they start thinking about how to promote their podcasts is spamming, or posting unsolicited advertisements in e-mails or on other people's forums or Web pages. The keyword is "unsolicited" – electronic equivalents of the junk mail you receive in your mailbox everyday.

The benefit of spamming as a promotional plan is obvious: If you plaster the Internet with links to your podcast feed, people will know about your podcast. However, the disadvantages might not be as obvious. People hate spam, and webmasters hate it when others post spam in their domains, very often because advertisements are what pay their salaries, and spammers are trying to get a free lunch.

It might not be apparent the first time you sit down alone in front of the microphone, but podcasting can be a surprisingly intimate medium. You are not starting your relationship with your listeners on the right foot if their initial impression of you is "spammer." If that does not make you stop, the second reason definitely should. The webmasters of forums and other Internet domains related to your topic are potentially your greatest allies in getting the word out about your podcast. One kind reference from them is easily worth a thousand unsolicited spam messages.

This is not to say that you cannot leverage the popularity of others into a larger audience pool; spam is just the wrong way to do it. Jeff McQuillan, of *ESL Pod*, one of the highest rated educational podcasts in the iTunes directory, does not put too fine a point on it: Podcasting is intimate, and the most common mistake he says he sees in amateur podcasters is the tendency to forget the relationship they have with their own listeners.

Social media

The first thing you should do when you set out to market your podcast is run a search for Facebook groups, Web forums, and LiveJournal communities associated with your topic. These are known as social media sites, or websites designed for the purpose of building communities. Ideally, you want these to pertain directly to your own niche, but if that is not possible, a broader, related topic is OK.

Again, resist the temptation to spam; for example, do not post a message like this: "Please go check out my podcast at feed://xxxx." You need to be subtler than that. Just jump into the conversations already going on or start your own and have a conversation about your topic. This should not be difficult. After all, you are planning to spend many hours of your life on this topic. If you cannot hold a few conversations about it with fellow enthusiasts, you need to go back to square one and choose another topic.

After you have been active in the forum, Facebook group, or LiveJournal community for a few weeks, people will see you in a positive light, and the reaction to the exact same post that would have brought down the wrath of your potential audience a few weeks ago will be radically different now. You will be a member of their community, and seeing your podcast go live will thrill them, especially if you have made a good impression. For this reason, you should begin this before you have said the first word into your microphone.

One thing in particular to look for on any social media sites you visit while trying to market your podcast is a "signature" feature. This feature allows you to automatically attach a short bit of HTML code to every post you make to that website. You are generally free to post anything you like in this space, provided you keep it very short. Most people use their signatures to post images, quotations they are fond of, or links to their own websites. This is generally not considered spam, even if the signature really is as blatant an advertisement as "Check out my podcast, *The Cross Country Cyclist*, here," with "here" being a link to your podcast.

Networking with other podcasters

It can be easy to fall into the trap of thinking of other podcasters in your topic as your competition, especially if you want to make money from your podcast. However, this mindset can deprive you of your greatest source of growth, especially in the early to middle stages in the life of your podcast.

If you have chosen a good niche, chances are there will not be more than a dozen podcasters reaching for an audience of thousands. And because it is not at all uncommon for an active podcast listener to subscribe to dozens of podcasts, you and your fellow podcasters have far more to gain by cooperating than competing.

This means networking, cultivating mutually beneficial relationships, will be a prime factor in the success of your podcast. Build and cultivate a relationship with others who podcast in your topic and related topics. Even if your networking, by some stroke of miserable luck, never provides a single new listener for your podcast, neglecting it means you are missing out on one of the great things about getting involved in the world of podcasting: meeting others who share your passion or your zeal.

Promos and quickcasts

Suppose Joe Podcaster has created his podcast about cross-country cycling. It is a good example of a narrowcasted market: There are only three or four other podcasts on the subject, and there is a substantial base of interest ready for him to tap into. After all, every cyclist is a potential cross-country cyclist. However, he cannot sit around waiting for listeners to find him in the iTunes directory.

Create a promo for your podcast as early as possible to gain listeners. A promo is a short advertisement for your podcast that you can exchange with fellow podcasters. Ideally, you would exchange promos with another podcaster in the same, or similar, subject and play them in the middle of the each other's podcast episode as a way to perform some quid pro quo promotion.

However, through Joe's networking on social media sites and forums in his topic or by personal acquaintance, he has already met another podcaster named Sarah Jones. Sarah produces a podcast on her own passion: mountain biking. It is not the same topic as Joe's podcast about cross-country cycling, but it is reasonable to believe that her mountain bikers might at least have an interest in Joe's podcast, and vice versa. Sarah hopes the cross-country audience Joe brings in will be interested in her show on mountain biking.

A bit of mutual promotion sounds like a win-win situation, so they agree to exchange a 30-second promo that they will each play, like an advertisement, at the beginning or end of the other's episodes for a few episodes. It might just play the show's theme music and invite listeners to run a search for the name of the show in iTunes.

A quickcast is very similar to a promo and serves the same function. Although a promo is like an advertisement, a quickcast is more like a guest appearance. In a quickcast, the podcaster does a short show, usually around one to five minutes long, which another podcaster agrees to add to his or her own feed or even place in the middle of one of his or her own episodes.

The result is the same: Two podcasters share each other with their listeners as a way to build their own listener base and the community spirit within their own groups.

Web rings

Your podcast is going to need a website to give it a permanent presence where your audience can meet, find out more about you, and check for news and other events that time constraints prevent you from mentioning in your podcast episodes. If you are going to have a website, you will need to see if there is already a Web ring for your topic. A Web ring is a special type of site that is used to chain together a collection of websites about a single topic. To contribute and be included in the Web ring, each website in the chain is expected to include a link to the next website in the ring somewhere prominently on its own Web page, usually next to a small banner for the Web ring itself.

Just like promos, quick-casts, and social media networking, Web rings are a way to build community spirit and grow your base of listeners. The more ways you can lead potential listeners to your website and your podcast, the faster your podcast will grow.

SEO

Search engine optimization (SEO) is a cross between marketing and computer science that focuses on finding ways, some legitimate and others dishonest, to boost a website's placement in a search engine's results.

When employed honestly, SEO techniques increase the efficiency of the Internet, help users find the content they are looking for, and help publishers (like you) get the word out to users. However, when employed dishonestly, SEO techniques undermine the value of the search engines themselves. Because of this, it is no surprise engineers at search engines like Google are always trying to sniff out and penalize those who employ deceitful SEO methods to get a short-term boost for their websites.

A particularly infamous example was BMW's experiment with dishonest, or black hat, SEO in 2006. The German car company had generated vast numbers of fake Web pages in order to trick the Google search engine into believing their home page was more popular than it really was. The result, far from being a boost in long-term traffic, was a public relations disaster after the company found its Web page banned from the Google search engine until its attempts to manipulate the search engine were mended and the company issued a statement to Google assuring it would not attempt it again in the future. Though many companies and books allege to teach you the ways to outsmart the search algorithms, the benefits of deceitful SEO are not worth it in the long run. *Chapter 11 discusses white hat, or honest, SEO.* This is not just because we like to be honest: even full-time SEO teams, like those at BMW, who dabble in underhanded SEO methods have found themselves losing out in the long run.

Advertising

Traditional advertising campaigns work, too. Rather than, or in addition to, spreading the word about your podcast through networking, social media, and word-of-mouth, a direct advertising plan would involve taking out Internet banner ads and commercial time in another podcast. You could also pay Google a few cents per click to have your podcast's website appear in the first three results of a search for specific keywords. *Chapter 11 discusses the routes of advertising available to your podcast and how to employ them successfully.*

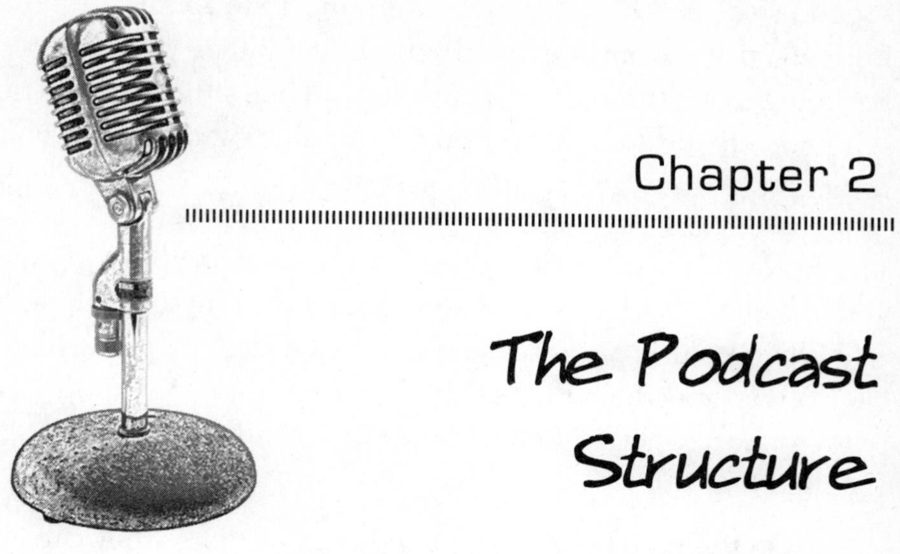

Chapter 2

The Podcast Structure

Podcasts are an open-ended way to distribute media, and you do not need to worry about fitting your content into a certain time slot or word count like publishers on television, radio, and newspaper are required to do every day. However, people do have some expectations about the way podcasts are structured.

Length

It is true that there are few technical limits as to how long you can make a podcast episode. But before you rush off to create your own eight-week podcast marathon, bear in mind that the average MP3 player can only hold a few hundred hours of audio total, and your listeners will not thank you for filling it all up with one show.

A good podcast length tends to be around 15 to 45 minutes. Any longer and it becomes increasingly unlikely that your listeners are going to get through an entire show in one sitting. But do not sell yourself short either, or you will be signing off just as your listeners are really getting into the show.

Where your show fits in that range will depend on your topic and your listeners, so remember your audience. Put some thought into when your is audience going to listen to your podcast and try to ascertain which type of listener tunes into your show. The following are a few different types of listeners that you might encounter:

- **On the go**: These people bought a headset so they can drive and talk at the same time (and have not taken it off since). They are the sales people, managers, and efficiency gurus among us. They will listen to your podcast, but only in their few spare moments. Fifteen minutes is the maximum, and you might want to stray on the low side and aim for around five.
- **Average**: These people are busy, but they do find time to let their hair down and take the headset off. They will also listen to your podcast in spare moments, but they have more of them — perhaps during a long commute or while working out. Fifteen to 30 minutes would be a good average podcast length.
- **Laid back**: Perhaps these listeners are students with more time on their hands (or students who like to listen to podcasts while studying), or maybe they just take life at their own pace. Either way, if you have reason to believe your audience is laid back, you might aim for your podcast to be around 45 minutes long.

Short of commissioning professional — and expensive — demographic research, there is no easy way to get absolutely accurate information about your listeners. For now, just picture your audience based on your knowledge of the topic. If you are not sure how to go about doing that, do not worry; people have a way of getting surprisingly vocal on the Internet. If your listeners start complaining on your website that your episodes seem to end before they begin, or that they seem to go on too long, you should adjust the length.

Of course, your topic might dictate the length for you. For example, a podcast on obscure, long-dead writers might have a minimum length forced on it by the simple fact that writers of the late 19th and early 20th century could be a bit long-winded. Even if the audience were considered "on the go," it would be impossible to fit the subject matter into a podcast shorter than 20 minutes.

If your topic requires episodes on the longer side but also has an audience unlikely to listen in one sitting, here are a few possible solutions:

- **Break it up.** Find a good place to break, and issue your podcast episode in two or three parts, labeled "Part One," "Part Two," and so on. This makes it explicit and clear to the audience what is going on. On the surface, this is an ideal solution, but it has serious problems. Many players, including the Apple iPods, will sort a podcast according to how recently it was downloaded, and that means a podcast that has been broken into parts will play in the wrong order, starting with the last episode and ending with the first, unless your listener manually chooses each episode in turn. Making matters worse, some podcatchers, like Apple's iTunes, will only download the most recent episodes if more than one comes online at a time. A listener who plugs in his or her MP3 player, hits the sync button, and walks off will be frustrated to discover later on that only the last part of a three-part episode downloaded.

- **Use natural stopping points within the podcast.** This ensures listeners are always walking around with a complete episode and will listen to the parts in order, while giving them natural places to start and stop should the episode run a little long for their schedule. Most players designed with podcasts in mind will be able to keep track of where the listener stopped during an episode. However, you need to take account in your script of where your audience is likely to stop, and ensure that the next segment opens smoothly enough to give a listener who might have been away for a week or more can get back on track. Natural stopping points also make a great place for advertisements or quickcasts from your affiliates. For example, the popular podcast This American Life always cuts their shows into three distinct acts.
- **Work on cutting the length.** To be blunt, your episodes might just be a little too long-winded. Take some time with a script and decide what can be cut to get your shows down to a more reasonable size.

Intros and Outros

For your first podcast, put some extra thought into your intros and outros, or the sounds that will play whenever your podcast

begins and ends, and any words you want to introduce and close your episodes with. These give your podcasts a consistent feel, and let your listeners ease into, and out of, each show. If these seem irrelevant, just consider your favorite radio or television programs. Talk shows always open and close with some sort of music and, on radio and television talk shows, an introduction by the host. Television sitcoms typically have a long establishment shot or sequence with music as an introduction.

If you are not convinced of the importance of a consistent intros and outros, take some time to think about how your audience is going to listen to your show. Most podcast listeners just hit the play button and let the MP3 player go through a list of their subscriptions. You do not want your listeners to think, "What is this?" when your podcast starts playing. As soon as someone hears your music and your trademark introduction to the show, he or she should know what to expect. Beyond the intros and outros that mark the beginning and end of the show, you might also need a consistent way to break the show up in the middle for advertisements, promos for other podcasters, or clearly identified segments. If you do decide to break your show into segments, you will want to make a short version of your intros and outros for each break as well. Do some research; watch your favorite shows, and listen to your favorite radio programs and podcasts. You will see a pattern that you can emulate. *You can read more about the practical side of doing this in Chapter 6 on post-production.*

Release Schedule

Television and radio stations have a pretty tall order to fulfill. They follow schedules that plan, down to the second, what will be broadcasted 24 hours a day, seven days a week. Programs starting late, running over, ending early, or just plain not being ready when the scheduled time arrives can lead to a disaster. As a podcast producer, you are spared a fair bit of that.

Because there is always a bit of lag between recording, releasing, and playing, being late or early on a podcast release can be measured in days rather than seconds. If you have set a goal of a ten-minute podcast, you do not need to stress out about hitting ten minutes, to the second, the way your colleagues working in radio and television do. At the same time, your listeners will quickly grow impatient if, week after week, month after month, they check their iPods for "Extreme Cross-Country Cycler" and there is never a new episode. Eventually, they will stop looking and you will see your subscription rates plummet. They will also grow frustrated if the length of the podcast ranges from a few minutes one week to a few hours the next.

The best schedule is a release period of every few days for a short podcast and every few weeks for a longer one. Feel free to adjust your schedule to suit how quickly you can produce episodes. Just remember to keep your release periods consistent, whether you choose to release one episode a week or one episode a month.

Podfading

Podfading is a term the podcasting community has adapted to describe the unfortunate tendency for new producers to create a new podcast, grab an audience of listeners, and flicker out. If you have ever browsed a podcast directory, you have probably seen a few casualties of podfading: shows starting out with regular updates before going silent for months or years at a time.

Preventing podfading is more an exercise in self-discipline than anything else, but a few ideas can deter a slow and painful death:

- **Choose the right topic.** Go with something that has thrilled you for a long time. The surest possible invitation to podfading is simply to start a podcast on a subject that will not sustain your own long-term interest. We all know how it feels: Some passions stay with us for a lifetime, but others only last a few months.
- **Stay ahead of schedule.** The first episode release is always easiest, and missing your release date for an episode is no exception. But podcasters get sick and day jobs have deadlines too, so try to keep a few episodes held in reserve in case life just gets in the way.
- **Make sure you can keep your current pace.** It is easy to release an episode daily in the early days of your podcast. It is your new and exciting hobby, after all. But before you commit to a daily release schedule, or even a weekly release schedule, ask yourself: Can you keep it up? Adopt a release schedule that fits your lifestyle. The last thing you want is to resent your podcast because it is taking time from your kids or resent your family because they are affecting your self-imposed release schedule.

Scripting

Have you ever found yourself lying in bed at night, replaying conversations in your head, and realizing hours too late that there was a clearer way to answer that question, a wittier way to make that point, or a funnier way to tell that joke?

It would be wonderful if life presented us with situations and conversations a few weeks in advance to give us the chance to choose our words carefully. Conversations would certainly be snappier, wittier, and more interesting. Fortunately, this can happen with your podcast – you just have to take the time to write a script.

There are three ways you can choose to go about scripting. Some rare and exceptional people, like Howard Stern, David Letterman, and the Robin Williams' character in "Good Morning, Vietnam" can work without a script. The vast majority of us are not wired to work that way, and if the temptation comes along to just plop down in front of the microphone and hit the record button, the result is usually something like this:

> "Welcome to the show! My name is Kevin Walker, and we are going to spend the next ten minutes talking about cross-country cycling.
>
> Umm.
>
> Right, so…cross-country cycling. Cross-country cycling is a sport. We all know that. Many people really like sports, like baseball, basketball. Umm. Football.
>
> Yeah.
>
> So, that was our show! See you again next week."

That recording should be promptly deleted and thrown in the recycle bin. The podcaster should be motivated to write a script after listening to an episode of "umms," "rights," and "yeahs." Of course, you might be one of the very few, a Robin Williams among us, who can sit down in front of a microphone without a script and talk coherently for hours. Some people just have that gift. The majority of aspiring podcasters will need the following sections, though.

The full script

When a full script is written, every word is written down ahead of time, usually along with some notes about how to speak them, such as where to pause for effect or which words to emphasize. A word-for-word script for the entire episode might be the best method for a podcast with a lone host.

This gives you extra time to find the best way to express the things you want to say, ask friends and family for feedback, and ensure that you always present your best to the listening world.

That does not mean you cannot stray off script. If you have an epiphany about a better way to put things mid-show, go for it. After all, no one else will ever see the script besides you.

Talking points

Sometimes it is just not possible to write down every word for a show in advance. You might have a co-host or two, and it can often be pretty difficult to get everyone together for the recording, much less for an hour or two of scripting beforehand, and the result rarely sounds natural. If a given show depends on an interview, the same situation applies: Few people worth interviewing are going to be content to sit down with you a few hours before the show and write a script for the whole thing in advance. Depending on your topic, you might also wish to do some live podcasting at a major event, like a convention dedicated to your topic. Live-event podcasting can be a great way to generate word-of-mouth promotion for your show among your listeners. Rhonda Rivera, host of *Ear on Careers*, emphasizes the importance of giving guests a copy of show notes and talking points so they can prepare and feel at ease when the microphone goes on.

Even in these situations, however, it is not wise to work off the top of your head. If nothing else, you need talking points, a list of anywhere from five to 20 things you intend to discuss during the course of the show. For an interview, these are the questions you want to make sure you ask. If you are trying to do a live podcast from some event, talking points might just be a list of topics you want to talk about during the course of the show. With co-hosts, they can simply be topics of conversation and a general outline of how long each conversation ought to last.

The purpose is to prevent the dreaded "umm," "yeah," and "right" – words that find themselves drifting into ordinary speech when people are left to fend for themselves. Any time you find yourself floundering for something to say or drifting too far off topic, look down and pull the discussion back to one of the talking points.

Ramble and edit

There is one way you can go without a script if you are feeling especially bold and have the time and discipline for it: a laid-back form of podcasting known as "ramble and edit."

With this philosophy, you sit back, hit the record button, and let your thoughts flow — pauses and all. If you think of a better way to say something a few minutes later, then just stop and say it. Later, sit down with editing software and spend some time cutting the bad and rearranging the good with some transitions and fresh recordings to bridge the gaps. A podcast that uses this to great effect is the *You Look Nice Today* podcast, a Seinfieldesque podcast in which the three hosts talk about everything, and nothing, in a series of hilarious 30-minute episodes. *Using editing software like GarageBand and Audacity is discussed in Chapters 5 and 6.*

Do not misinterpret this as a shortcut to avoid scripting. Even with a full script in hand, you are going to spend at least a few minutes in post-production for every minute you record, and every step away from that is going to require more time editing out mistakes in order to produce a quality show. With ramble and edit, you might find yourself having to re-record whole segments just to get the recordings to match up, which means, in practice, the ramble and edit takes a great deal longer than it would take to just write and record a script.

But if you are the type who can talk naturally off the top of your head and cannot fill a page to save your life, it can be an alternative to script writing.

Choosing a scripting method

Which method you choose depends, more than anything else, on your personality. Some people can talk for hours on end without rambling off topic, stuttering, or stopping to think, and others deeply wish scripting were an option in ordinary day-to-day conversation. Most of us fall somewhere in between. However you script your show, no one will ever see the script or know it exists. Your podcast will be judged by what you have to say and how you say it, and only you know whether you are the sort of person that will say it best with a detailed script in hand, a few jotted ideas on a napkin, or just off the top of your head.

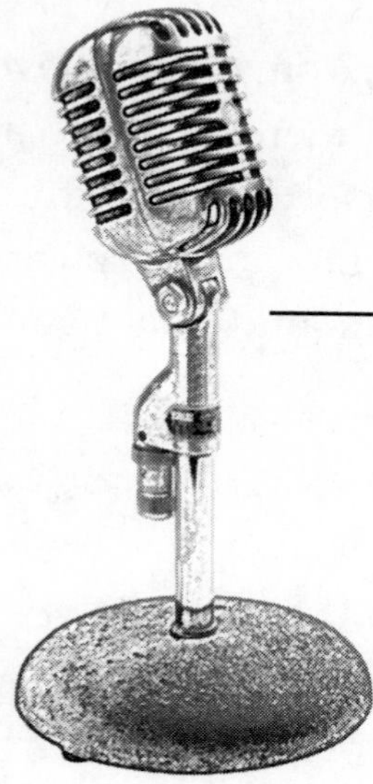

Chapter 3

The Studio

Choosing your studio is the second most important decision you will make for your podcast. The best studio in the world will not save a boring show, and a great show will probably have at least a few listeners, even if it is recorded with a $2 microphone under a busy highway overpass. But, you want to put your best foot forward. The first thing people are going to use to judge your podcast, before they judge what you have to say or how you say it, is sound quality, which depends on your studio and your microphone. You never get a second chance to make a good first impression.

In a way, the big dollar professionals have it easy: They get to start from scratch and build an entire room designed from the ground up for the sole purpose of recording audio and another just for editing. Chances are you do not have the deep pockets that would be needed for the task of building an entire studio from scratch. You have to make do with what you already have in your own home and office, but that is OK. You are on a level playing field with most of the podcasters out there. Some go all out and equip an entire room with the best gear they can afford, while others work out of bathrooms, basements, and even cars. At the end of the day, all that matters is the sound quality and what you have to say.

Things to Think About When Choosing a Studio

The last chapter focused largely on what to say during your podcasts. That is probably the least of your problems. In the early days of a podcast, the technical aspects will probably pose the greatest obstacle to most aspiring podcasters who lack a background in sound engineering or computers.

Acoustics

Acoustics is the science that studies sound and how it interacts with its environment. You do not need to go back to your high school physics class to make a successful podcast, but a little acoustics fundamentals will not hurt when it comes to choosing your studio.

Sound is generated any time a substance vibrates, and different substances transmit sound in different ways. Generally, we hear sound as it travels through the air, but air is not really the best substance for sound to travel through. Liquids and solids both transmit sound better than air. You can test this yourself in a couple of ways. If you submerge your ears in the bathtub, you

might notice a sudden increase in volume of the air conditioner. If you use a lake or beach near your home that allows both swimmers and motorboats, the engines of boats on the horizon that are barely audible above the surface are amplified dramatically underwater. Finally, you can press your ear to a door or wall to hear the person in the next room — just make sure they know you are listening.

Nevertheless, the volume of sound decreases every time the sound moves from one material to another, say from air to a wall. This is called transmission loss. The more solid and less flexible the barrier, the more isolation it provides from noise outside. The typical wall in an American home can provide about 35 decibels (dB) worth of isolation from the outside world. Studios built specifically for recording use special recording methods to isolate them from up to 60 dB of sound.

It is unlikely you have the luxury of building a custom room to be used solely for recording, but you can do a few things to make your chosen studio the best acoustics environment it can be.

Spend some time soundproofing your windows and doors. Any corridor of air between your studio and the environment outside will increase the ability of noise to penetrate. Not to mention, you will also see some decreases in your heating and cooling costs.

Some builders reserve their solid doors for the exterior of the house, and use cheaper, hollow doors on the interior. Consider replacing the interior door to your home studio with a more solid door. And, if your studio has an external window, cover it with drapes, the heavier the better. These will reduce the amount of noise able to penetrate from outside the studio.

Carpeted floors, upholstered furniture, and – if you have the money – soundboard and acoustic tiling on walls and ceilings cannot reduce the amount of noise coming into the room itself, but these items can absorb is the noise already in the room by cutting down on echos.

Ambient noise

As a podcaster working on a budget, ambient noise is your single greatest enemy. It refers to everything in the house and outside that make noise, which is more than you might suspect and includes air conditioners, ceiling fans, pets, traffic, outdoor noise, and family members or roommates elsewhere in the house. The sheer quantity of noise that envelopes the average home can be a shock to the new podcaster, because the human ear has a strange knack for slowly tuning out common and constant sounds like water heaters, ceiling fans, or the quiet squeaks of an office chair. Unfortunately, microphones do not share this ability and have the annoying habit of picking up every minute sound.

Radio stations and recording studios spend thousands, if not more, on eliminating these sounds, but you will need to use a variety of other techniques to minimize the ambient noise around you without breaking the bank before hitting the record button. This is called minimizing your noise floor, the amount of sound picked up by the microphone when there should be dead silence. Unless you have the money, creativity and a little awareness are your best friends. If you already have your microphone and a good pair of (non-noise-canceling) headphones, nothing beats flipping the microphone on, turning the volume on the headphones up, and just listening for any sound. You might hear foot traffic in the house, pets, cars driving by outside, air conditioners, water heaters, a refilling toilet, and even the wind. Once you hear it, do what you can to get rid of it. Many podcasters put blankets over windows while they record or even build tents in their livings rooms with heavy quilts. You may need to put pets outside or in another part of the house during recording sessions. If your family is sympathetic, you can have a low-noise period. Otherwise, you can just record while they are away. Just keeping an open ear, before and during your recordings, will go a long way to lowering the noise floor and improving the quality of the show.

Sets

Video podcasters have an extra concern to worry about: They need sets to serve as backdrops, and they need to put some thought into lighting. You will know based on your show what sort of set suits the show. Some video podcasters are content just to run the camera while they speak into the microphone. This is especially common with v-loggers on sites like YouTube. Others prefer a more elaborate set design or recording outdoors.

Budget Studios

There are a number of options podcasters have used to get a high-quality sound while keeping the savings account safe, ranging from bathrooms to basements. If you are doing an audio podcast, the studio does not have to be beautiful or impressive. All that matters is the sound, so use your ears, not your eyes, to find the perfect location.

Bathroom

The bathroom has been an old standby for home-recorders since parodist Weird Al Yankovic recorded one of his first parody songs, "My Bologna," in a public restroom across the hall from his university's student radio station.

The advantages of recording in the bathroom can be surprisingly numerous. This relatively small room can provide a natural reverb, or mild echo effect, and the tiling used in the bathroom can function as passable stand-in for the acoustic tiling used in professional studios. In addition, most bathrooms are situated in the center of the house and sealed off from outside sources of noise.

There are some disadvantages to working in a bathroom, though. Besides the obvious fact that water does not mix well with microphones, computers, and other essential (and expensive) electrical equipment, it is also not an environment designed for working. Family members and roommates will probably be a great deal less supportive of your podcasting venture if it means they have to "hold it in" during recording sessions. It also has its own sources of ambient noise, including the water basin in the toilet; the water heater, which is usually nearby; and as was mentioned in the acoustics section, the sounds from water pipes, which travel a long way. If you live in an apartment, these sounds can be out of your control.

Finally, the reverb might be a little too much. A little reverb can add a pleasant depth and warmth to make your voice sound more natural, but you can easily cross the line into having too much. This might take some trial and error, so take some time to listen to yourself through the microphone and headphones. The best reverb level is a difficult thing to describe and has a definite "You

will know it when you hear it" feel. If it sounds like "depth," it is a good reverb. If it sounds like "echo," it is too much.

Basement

If your home has one, the benefits a bathroom provides can be gained from heading downstairs to the basement. The subterranean atmosphere will cut down on noise from outside dramatically, and if your budget can accommodate it, it may be the best place for a little self-installed acoustic tiling. However, this environment has one big disadvantage: Although ambient noise like sound and wind from outdoors are certain to be filtered out, footsteps from above are almost certain to be audible in your recordings. If you can wait for an empty house or until everyone is asleep, the basement can be a good option.

Home office

Podcasting will require a working atmosphere for writing a script and editing the audio file, so you might consider setting up your recording studio in you home office, which should be furnished so you can work comfortably. It will take some special precautions to lower the noise floor. Air conditioning vents should be closed while you work, and you might even need to turn the air conditioner off completely during recordings to cut down on the noise of the rushing air during your podcast. Pets should be placed as far away from the studio as possible, and family members need to cooperate to keep the noise down.

Closet

Some podcasters choose to record out of a walk-in closet. It is private and, like a bathroom, is a small enough space that you are likely to get some reverb in your recordings. But, just like a bathroom, the reverb may be a bit too much, and even after you have cleared the closet, it might not be the best work environment. Before you start pulling out the clothes and boxes, make sure your walk-in closet has a power outlet and enough space to hold a computer, microphone, and comfortable chair.

Car

No, it is not recommended you juggle your podcasting in between driving, using your cell phone, and watching your built-in DVD player. Do not do anything dangerous. However, some podcasters have gotten their start from a (parked) car.

Besides the fact that this lets a busy professional squeeze out a fast episode during lunch break, cars are not too shabby as far as a budget studio is concerned. They are usually designed to seal out a great deal of outside noise, and they offer another confined area where you can find just the right balance of reverb. If you can park in a remote area away from other traffic, you might discover that you already have your own multi-thousand dollar recording studio.

The disadvantages are palpable, though. Along with the usual caveat that it is easy to get too much reverb in a confined space, few cars are designed to power computers, microphones, and mixing equipment. And, of course, you cannot record with the engine running, so that means no air conditioning. You might not care, but in some parts of the country and at certain times of year,

you might be wondering which will die from the heat first: your equipment or you.

Blanket

You do not have a basement and you skipped the section on bathrooms because you do not like the idea of putting your new $200 condenser microphone so close to water. You are envious of the people who have professional vocal booths, but you do not envy the price tag. You do not have a walk-in closet, it is 100 degrees outside, and in the quietest room of your house, you can still hear the rush of traffic on the nearby freeway. You are not completely out of options.

With a heavy winter blanket and a little creativity, you can set up your own vocal booth in the middle of your living room. Just hang the blanket over one wall from a few feet of clothesline and face it as your record. The thick fabric will reduce noise from outside, especially if you hang it over a window, and it will cut down on the echo of your walls just enough to generate a nice reverb, making it a great substitution for a vocal booth.

Microphone Terminology

Your choice in microphone is the second most important decision you will make about your podcast — after your choice of recording location. The worst thing you can do, and the surest way to find yourself getting frustrated, is to simply take any random microphone off the shelf at your local computer store. Take a few minutes to go through this crash course in microphone technology, so you know what you are looking for before you step inside the store.

Remember, it is always better to take a little time and ensure your first purchase is the right purchase rather than to take a second trip to the store to spend more money trying to correct a mistake. This might get technical, so check the Glossary of this book if you cannot remember what a microphone term means.

Frequency response

Microphones each have their own frequency response, a measurement of how sensitive the microphone is to incoming sound of different frequencies. The perfect microphone would be one with a flat frequency response, or one that records high, middle, and low pitch sounds equally well. Unfortunately, nearly all microphones have a tendency to exaggerate sounds with a higher pitch, so look at the frequency response chart for each mic you are considering and compare it with others in your price range.

When reading a frequency response chart, look for two things. First, the flatter the line on the chart, the more accurately the microphone will represent the sounds it records without exaggerations in pitch. No chart will be perfectly flat, and those microphones that are closest to having a flat frequency response will generally cost more, but the flatter you can go on your budget, the better off you will be.

Bear in mind as well that the manufacturer might not use a simple, linear scale for the chart. It is not uncommon for frequency charts to be published with a logarithmic scale. This mathematical trick allows the manufacturer to put more information on the

chart, but at the same time, it can make the microphone look as if it had a dramatically flatter frequency response than it really has. Be sure to check the numbers on the vertical axis of the chart. If they ascend at the same rate, for example 0, 10, 20 dB all the way up the chart, the chart is using a linear scale. However, if the numbers grow more quickly, for example, 0, 1, 10, 100, up the chart then it is using a logarithmic scale, and the chart will look flatter than normal.

Second, you want to check the response range for the microphone. On a frequency response chart, the curve will begin at a low frequency and abruptly end at another, higher frequency. For example, a given microphone's frequency response curve might begin at 40 hertz (Hz) and end at 17 kilohertz (kHz), or 17,000 Hz. For this microphone, any sound lower than 40 Hz or higher than 17 kHz will not be recorded at all.

An excellent microphone will have a frequency response beginning at 20 Hz and working up to 20 kHz. However, with post-production work, even a microphone with a range from 60 Hz to 16 kHz can get the job done for a podcaster trying to watch his or her budget.

Microphone Types

All microphones use some mechanism to translate the vibrations in the air that transfer sound into an electrical impulse. However, no microphone perfectly captures the sound around it. The precise method the microphone uses can and does have subtle effects on what is recorded.

Dynamic microphones

Most of the microphones available in a computer shop for video chat are dynamic microphones, as are most microphones used by reporters or karaoke machines. In these microphones, the incoming sound produces a vibration in a thin sheet of metal inside the mic, known as the diaphragm. Pressed against the diaphragm is a bit of coiled wire and a magnet. As the diaphragm vibrates, the coiled wire shakes, and this shaking motion, with the magnet nearby, produces an electric current that is later reconstructed into a sound wave.

If you are familiar with the construction of speakers, this might sound familiar. Dynamic microphones are basically loudspeakers working in reverse: Instead of an incoming electric current causing a vibration in the diaphragm that produces sound waves, the sound waves shake the diaphragm to produce the current.

Though they are generally the cheapest microphones available, they are not without their advantages, the most significant being their durability. Some microphone types can be ruined by the jostling involved in passing them back and forth during a question and answer session, but a solid dynamic microphone is designed to handle rougher environments. Not that you should feel free to bang your dynamic microphone up against the desk, but if you are going to be doing lots of interviews, outdoor podcasts, or travel with your microphone, it is good to know you will not sit down for post-production and discover a thick layer of distortion (or worse) covering your entire show.

However, you usually get what you pay for, and your typical dynamic microphone is going to suffer when it comes to frequency

response compared to a typical condenser microphone. More specifically, dynamic microphones tend to dramatically exaggerate the volume of high-frequency, high-pitched sounds coming into it and ignore lower frequency, lower-pitch sounds. So, even if you have James Earl Jones's voice, there is a limit to how much of that beautiful bass is going to show up in a recording made on a dynamic microphone.

Dynamic microphones are the cheapest variety, but there is a broad range of quality and price. The cheapest dynamic mic can go for about $2 new, but it is not recommended for your podcast. A more reasonable dynamic microphone can be had for between $5 and $50, but some of the best will run you upward of $300.

Condenser microphones

Condenser microphones are a substantial step up from a dynamic microphone, with a broader, flatter frequency range than their dynamic cousins. That means sounds that are higher and lower in pitch will be represented more accurately in the final recording.

A condenser microphone works by placing two metal plates together just inside the microphone with only a short gap separating them. The plates are connected to an electrical current arriving from outside the microphone. The front plate serves as the diaphragm, just as in the dynamic microphone, and as the front plate vibrates, the distance between the two plates changes, and this motion creates an electrical current that can be translated into a sound wave.

If you are familiar with electrical engineering, you will probably be saying to yourself, "I know that – that is a capacitor!" And, you would be right. The word "condenser" is simply an old-fashioned version of the word "capacitor" used in modern electrical engineering.

They are not without their disadvantages, however. They are more expensive. The cheapest condensers go for $60, but expect to pay upward of $100 for quality. They are also notoriously fragile and especially sensitive to loud noise. A dynamic microphone dropped on the floor would likely not suffer any loss in sound quality, but a condenser that falls to the floor would most likely be hopelessly ruined. And though a few condenser microphones have their own battery, most require an external power source in order to function.

Microphone Pick-up Patterns

As if it were not enough to divide microphones by the type of technology used to produce them, microphones are also categorized by their pick-up pattern, which is how the microphone will treat sounds coming from different directions when it records them.

Omnidirectional

Omnidirectional microphones record sound from all directions equally, and they usually have a rounded, foam head that makes them look like an ice cream cone. These types of microphones can be great for live music or

recording in a situation where it is impractical for each person speaking to have his or her own microphone.

They suffer from one major flaw, making them a poor choice for most podcasters: They tend to record ambient noise more dramatically then other microphone types.

Unidirectional

Compared to the snow-cone look of omnidirectional microphones, unidirectional microphones usually have a flat top without the foamy covering. Omnidirectional microphones pick up noise from everywhere around them indiscriminately, but unidirectional microphones are their polar opposite. These microphones record audio coming from one direction and one direction only. For podcasters, this translates into a dramatic reduction in ambient noise.

Unfortunately, unidirectional microphones are not a podcaster's dream mic either. The same feature is also their downfall. Unidirectional microphones are so good at sealing out sounds from other directions that even a shaking of the head or adjusting of a seat position causes dramatic variations in volume.

Cardioid

The cardioid family of microphones occupies the middle ground. Cardioid microphones reject sound from the rear and most of the noise from the sides of the microphone. Allowing some of the noise from the sides in lets podcasters adjust their seat naturally or move their head while they speak without worrying about dramatic volume differences.

They tend to be more expensive than their unidirectional cousins, so if you are starting your podcast on a shoestring budget, you might want to go for a unidirectional mike and just remember to keep its deficiencies in mind as you record.

Supercardioid and hypercardioid

Supercardioid and hypercardioid microphones are small branches of the cardioid family. Though simple cardioids completely block sound coming from behind the microphone, these microphones record sound from the rear, but at a dramatically lower volume. This keeps ambient noise out of your recording, while allowing a little bit of the sound of your voice to bounce back into the microphone from the opposing wall and generate a pleasant reverb.

Other Important Microphone Features

Knowing the advantages and disadvantages of dynamic and condenser microphones, as well as the major pick-up patterns, arms you with most of the information you will need to make an intelligent microphone choice based on your budget. But, the following sections offer a few more terms you might run into while shopping for your microphone and discuss how they will affect your podcast.

Dynamic range

Although frequency response tells you how much the microphone exaggerates or neglects certain pitches, the dynamic range gives you an idea of the loudest and softest sounds that your microphone can capture. If a sound is louder than this range, the sound will be increasingly distorted. If quieter, it will fail to record at all, or more precisely, the sound made by the microphone itself will overpower the recorded sound.

For example, if a microphone's data sheet says it has a dynamic range of 110 dB, it means there is a 110 dB difference between the loudest and quietest sounds the microphone can record. The human ear can register a range of about 120 dB before the sound itself becomes painful, so this microphone would cover the full range of sounds likely to appear in your podcast.

How much you care about this number will depend on what you intend to do with your podcast. If you expect the content of your podcast to remain at a normal, conversational tone, you can tolerate a microphone with a lower dynamic range. If you want to ensure a faithful reproduction of both loud and quiet sounds — for a dramatized radio show or a show about classical music, for example — you might want a higher range.

Do not think you can forget dynamic range once you have purchased your microphone. Media files like MP3 and Ogg Vorbis have a dynamic range as well, and if you are producing a podcast with wild swings in volume levels, you will need to ensure you encode your files with a suitable dynamic range available during post-production as well.

Choosing a Microphone

This might seem like a lot to take in, but remember it is actually very simple. After all the talk about pick-up patterns, condensers, and frequency response charts, one thing really matters: How does it sound? If you already have an old dynamic mic sitting around that you use for voice chat, do a sample recording with it and listen to it play back.

Be your own worst critic. Remember, your listeners are going to spend hours listening to this. They do not want to be distracted by pops and static. They should feel like they are listening to another person in the same room and not over a cheap intercom.

You will want the best mic you can afford, but there is no such thing as a perfect microphone. Expensive condensers will have a better sound than dynamics, but if your podcast will include many interviews or recording on the move, your money would be better spent on a quality dynamic mic, rather than a fragile condenser that will break as it is passed back and forth during the first interview.

If you cannot decide which direction to go, there is no reason to limit yourself to one microphone. With a mixing board or custom sound card, the part of the computer's hardware designed to read from microphones, you can have as many microphones as you want active at once. It is not unheard of for a podcaster to have a favorite condenser mic while keeping a few dynamic mikes around for interviews and other situations.

Remember that you get what you pay for. On average, condensers are going to deliver a better sound, but there is such a thing a

low-quality condenser microphone, and you would be a fool to choose a $20 condenser over a quality dynamic microphone.

CASE STUDY: YOU WILL BE JUDGED BY YOUR SOUND

Corey Koehler, host
Musicgoat Melting Pot
www.planetcorey.com
ckoehlerhw@gmail.com

Corey Koehler started *Musicgoat Melting Pot* in his basement in 2006 as a way to share some of his favorite music. He said that his favorite part is when the microphone is on and he gets to just play the music and talk about it with his listeners. He works alone now, but used to have a fantasy football podcast with a co-host and said that, when working with another host, communication is key. Everyone needs to share notes and outlines so that, once the microphone is on, no one is left stuttering.

When asked about common mistakes he sees other podcasters making, he immediately cited poor sound quality and pointed out that many hosts never seem to directly engage their audiences. He recommends giving a "call to action," asking listeners, in every episode, to subscribe and share the podcast with their friends.

His studio is his basement, and he record on a professional Heil PR-40 dynamic microphone. He uses Audacity, along with the CastBlaster program for Windows. His advice for new podcasters: "Get a good microphone."

Headphones

You want a quality set of headphones to record your podcasts, and some dedicated podcasters even spend more on headphones than microphones. Although a good microphone helps ensure that what goes into the machine is a high-quality sound, your headphones are your line of quality control. The only way to detect problems in your podcast is by listening, and the better your headphones reproduce the sound, the better off you will be. By wearing headphones during your recording session, you are always listening to what the microphone hears, as opposed to what you hear. The difference can be dramatic, and wearing a good pair of headphones during all your recording sessions allows you to detect any problems as soon as they occur, which can spare you a great deal of work later.

Before you rush out and buy a pair, there is one feature to avoid at all costs. Noise-reduction headphones contain a circuit that tries to sort out unwanted noise and static from the audio coming into the headphones and deliver only the pure audio to the listener's ears. For listening to music and podcasts, it is hard to beat the quality of a good pair of noise-reduction headphones.

Noise-reduction headphones

But for recording, noise-reduction headphones pose a problem. If there is noise being recorded in your podcast, you want to know about it as early as possible — preferably before you have even begun to speak. The last thing you want is to spend 30 to 45 minutes recording and thinking, "Wow, this sounds good today," only to discover that your entire podcast is set against the background of a whirring ceiling fan that your headphones hid from you, leaving you with the uncomfortable choice of starting over, trying to strip the noise out in post-production, or publishing a subpar episode. Noise and your own mistakes are the primary things you are listening for during your recording sessions. Keep

an eye out for headphones advertised as studio or monitor headphones and you should be safe from noise-reduction.

Monitor headphones

The second rule is simple: You want a pair of closed-ear headphones, which surround the entire ear. You will want to avoid ear buds, or headphones that take the form of small buds pushed into the ears. Ear buds can be great for podcast listeners on the go, but they do not do a good job of blocking external sounds. While you are recording your podcast, you do not want to spend any time trying to figure out if any ambient noise is coming from the headphones (and therefore being recorded) or getting through the headphones from your environment.

There are other types of headphones besides closed-ear and ear buds, such as the closed-back or semi-open headphones. Listeners can strive to find a middle ground between closed-ear headphones and ear buds, but podcast recorders have no choice. Closed-ear headphones are the only option.

Once you have narrowed your choices to closed-ear, non-noise-canceling headphones, your selection is fairly open. More expensive headphones will produce a truer and more faithful sound and, perhaps more importantly, help you pinpoint sources of ambient noise that you might not have realized existed. As long as you meet these two requirements, you should be in good territory with your headphones, and spending more than $50 would be overkill on a podcast that consists mostly of speaking. However, if you plan on producing a fair bit of music for your own podcast, the sky is the limit, and the headphones are right up there next to the microphones in terms of importance.

Choosing a Computer

Chances are you already have a computer and, no matter what type of computer it is, it will be fine for capturing and editing the audio for your podcast. If you have complete freedom with your choice, then there is no question which computer is ideal: Most new Apple Mac computers come with the GarageBand® and iMovie® software that is ideal for starting audio and/or video podcasts. These programs cost $79 as part of the iLife suite if bought separately. Of course, you can produce your podcast on any Windows® machine using the free and open-source program Audacity or commercial programs like Adobe Audition, which have similar features to GarageBand and iMovie. However, you will be losing a great deal of the ease that comes with Apple software like GarageBand.

There is no need to go out and buy a new computer to begin your podcast. You only need to keep a few basic principles in mind, which include:

- **Disk Space:** You will distribute your podcasts using MP3 or Ogg Vorbis audio files. These formats use between 0.5 and 3 megabytes per minute of audio, depending on the quality level used when at creation. However, you will want to keep a lossless copy of your recordings around for a while, and these can often take up around 10 megabytes per minute. That might not sound like much, but it adds up to over half a gigabyte for every hour of audio.

- **Processor speed**: Audacity has the lowest processor requirements and will work with an ancient 300 megahertz (MHz) processor, but the faster your processor, the snappier your post-production work will be. Nothing can get old faster than having to wait for the computer to catch up to your every move. Although the processor will not be a bottleneck for an audio podcast, video podcast work is another story, and you will want a 2.0 gigahertz (GHz) processor or faster to keep from pulling your hair out while trying to work with your video.
- **RAM**: Random-access memory (RAM) is the part of your computer that is responsible for keeping track of the information your computer is using to do its job. You can think of it almost like your computer's attention span. The more RAM you have, the better. Although Audacity will work with as little as 128 megabytes, it recommends at least 2 gigabytes. This will never put a strain on your podcast, but greater amounts will help the processor keep your post-production work snappy. Chances are, your computer already has enough RAM to handle everything you will do in your podcast, but more is always better.
- **Sound card**: The sound card is the part of your computer responsible for handling the input and output of sound. If you are plugging your microphone straight into the sound card, then you may want to invest $30-$50 to upgrade the sound card. Alternatively, many microphones use USB as their interface to the computer, and these bypass the sound card altogether. You can tell the difference pretty easily; the inputs for a sound card look like standard inputs for a headphone or microphone on a

stereo, while a USB microphone will use the same plug as a mouse or keyboard.

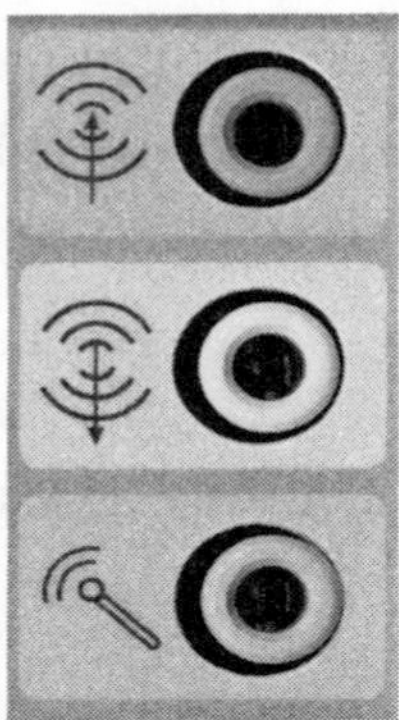
Sound card input

USB port

Optional Equipment

The essential equipment for your podcast is a good set of closed-ear, non-noise-canceling headphones, a good microphone, and a computer. However, the equipment discussed next will further improve the quality of your podcast.

Pop filter

Certain sounds produced by the human voice, especially the "P" sound, will create a rush of air that flies out of the mouth and into the microphone, creating an exaggerated popping sound in the recording. These are known as plosives. To combat this, professional studios place a wire circle filled with mesh, called a pop filter, between the speaker and the microphone to catch the rush of air before it is recorded. They can cost anywhere from $15 to $200;

however, many crafty podcasters never get around to buying a pop filter. They simply make their own out of panty hose and clothes hangers. These cheap pop filters will get the job done, but they also tend to subdue high-frequency, high-pitch sounds before they reach the microphone, and the most expensive pop filters cut down on that problem noticeably.

Mixing board

Most computers not built for audio mixing have a single port for a microphone. A mixing board combines all the inputs from your various microphones, music, and audio sources into one signal that you can plug into your computer. In addition to this function, most contain knobs and dials for each track that allow you to change the volume and stereo position of your different inputs to achieve a good mix.

For example, podcasters that take callers might have one channel on the mixer for their microphone, one channel for the phone, another channel for the guest, and a final channel for backup music and effects. If they have problem callers, they can reduce the volume of their voice, or mute them entirely, with one change of a dial. Fading music in or out from a CD player can be achieved the same way.

A simple podcasting setup with a single host on a microphone will likely not need a mixer. Many of the functions of mixers, such as theme music that fades in and out, can be done simply — and freely — with Audacity or GarageBand.

Compressor

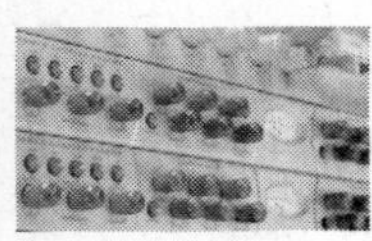

A compressor is a hardware device that attempts to keep the volume steady during a recording. If the volume of the recording suddenly drops, the compressor will increase the amplification to suit. Similarly, if the recording gets suddenly louder, the compressor will decrease it. A recording program, such as Audacity or GarageBand, can achieve the same effect.

However, there is one major reason to go with a hardware compressor. Because of the way digital audio is stored on a computer, it has a limited dynamic range. That range is fine for most tasks, but a dramatic rise to a very high volume can overwhelm the limits of the audio format and create distortion that a software compressor will not be able to correct. Therefore, if you expect dramatic changes to a very high volume during your podcast, you will want to invest in a hardware compressor to take the edges off and ensure that both loud and quiet sound is recorded without distortion. Many mixing boards have built-in compressors, so if you decide to purchase one or the other, finding one of these combo boards can be a useful investment.

Vocal booth

A vocal booth is like a small tent specifically designed to seal off the microphone from the outside world and its ambient noise. They can cost anywhere from $300 to $3,000, but if you are serious about podcasting and have deep pockets, they can be a worthwhile investment for your show. However, be sure you try some less drastic measures first, such as those described on the section on acoustics earlier in this chapter.

Chapter 4

Recording and Editing Software

The software side of your recording studio is just as important the hardware side. A wide variety of software tools can help you get your show out of your head and onto the Internet, and it would be impossible to cover all of them. Your preference will depend on everything from your own individual tastes to which features you need and what hardware equipment you already have. This book will primarily focus on two applications: the commercial GarageBand for Mac OS X and the free program Audacity for Windows, Macs, and Linux, but there are literally hundreds of others, and once you have learned one, you might want to investigate a few others until you find the right one for you. As you will see in the tutorials over the next few chapters for GarageBand and Audacity, each program generally functions the same way, and any skills you pick up in one will be easily transferred to any other podcasting software.

GarageBand

GarageBand is the all-in-one recording and podcasting studio that comes with Apple's iLife® home suite and usually comes free with a new Mac computer. If you have your choice, GarageBand is the best option for the new podcaster. Powerful post-production tools and special effects are provided that can cost thousands to produce with hardware. Mixing multiple tracks and editing audio is easy with the interface. It even comes with hundreds of royalty-free music samples that you can use as intros and outros for your podcast. The greatest disadvantage to using GarageBand is that it is only available for Apple computers running their Mac OS X operating system. If you already have a Mac, it is great and few podcasters would recommend buying a brand new computer with an unfamiliar operating system; that money would be better spent on microphone and headphone upgrades.

Audacity

The cheapest option available for your podcasting needs is Audacity. This free audio recording application has the necessary features, but in a much more complex interface. A few technical aspects of audio recording that GarageBand takes for granted on your behalf are exposed to you by Audacity. This grants the user a little more freedom than GarageBand, but it could have disastrous consequences for users unfamiliar with many of the technical aspects of how audio is stored on a computer. For example, it is possible to combine two recordings, stored on the computer with different settings, and get unintentional "chipmunk" style high-pitched voices in the result. Audacity is free and powerful, but it might not be worth it for you if GarageBand is an option.

For the Pros

Although this book confines its focus on how to achieve tasks in GarageBand and Audacity, there are a few types of industrial-level software that professionals use in the recording and broadcast industry. If you have deep pockets, the expertise, and the desire to create a state-of-the-art podcast, you cannot beat the features of programs like Cubase®, Apple Loops®, and Adobe Soundbooth®.

File Formats

Most podcasts are distributed using the nearly ubiquitous MP3 format. However, there are alternatives to this format, as well as a series of technical decisions to be made no matter which format you choose.

Audio and video formats

Entire books have been written on the technical details of converting light and sound into something a computer can store, transmit, and replay, but podcasters do not need to get too wrapped up in the details. They simply need to understand a few basic principles.

For one, podcasts are nearly always distributed using one of many formats that share one characteristic: They all use lossy compression. It turns out that it takes a huge amount of disc space to store and a lot of bandwidth, the amount of information that can flow through the network, to transmit sound and video in pristine perfection. To deal with this problem, sophisticated computer programs have been created that attempt to throw away information that people will not notice is missing.

It can be hard at first to see how this could work, but imagine the following scene in your head: You are in New Orleans for the biggest party in America: Mardi Gras. A parade is winding its way down the street. Every float is blasting music. Louder music is wafting down from every window. Firecrackers are going off. Someone is shouting at his friend down the street. Someone else is shouting at a stranger in a window. A few people just seem to be shouting for the sake of shouting. About 20 feet away, a cat meows.

In the tidal wave of sound that is New Orleans during Mardi Gras, no one will notice the cat, even if they listen to a recording of the parade a thousand times. But, the "meow" sound is still there, and more importantly, a microphone would still pick it up, so it is still taking up space in the recording of the Mardi Gras parade.

The software for lossy compression would throw away the cat's meow by calculating that the human ear would not notice such a quiet sound within such a loud environment, but that is not the only trick lossy compression uses. In music, if two similar notes are playing at same time, the lossy compression software simply combines them into one. The process is complex and involves enough math to make even a certified math whiz's head spin. If you have ever listened to music on an MP3 player, such as the iPod, you realize the success of the MP3 form of lossy compression. The typical MP3 file reduces the raw sound information to about one-tenth or even one-fiftieth of its original size.

For example, a movie is thousands and thousands of still photographs taken very quickly, usually between 25 and 72 times per second, and displayed again at the same speed to the viewers. Even though only still pictures are being used, they are being shown so quickly that the audience sees motion.

Even this is a low-tech form of lossy compression, and anything that happened in the intervening twenty-fifth of a second is never recorded. Most of the time, it is impossible for the human eye to notice. Some things happen so quickly, however, that an ordinary camera cannot capture them. For example, it is impossible to record something like a bullet leaving a gun on an ordinary movie camera. A single frame of ordinary camera film has an exposure time of around four-hundredths of a second. In that time, most bullets will have traveled at least 25 feet.

Nonetheless, 25 frames per second is still a lot of information, and the result is still too large to fit on a DVD or even on a Blu-ray Disc. A feature-length movie, at DVD-quality and recorded at a speed of 25 frames per second, would still require around 118 gigabytes, or 26 DVDs, to store without any further lossy compression. If you were downloading a movie without lossy compression, you would have to change discs every three and a half minutes, and even a two-minute trailer would take hours to download.

What information is thrown away when it comes time to squeeze a video onto a DVD, Blu-ray disc, or into a podcast? At the most basic level, this is easier to come to grips with than audio compression. Things like the beating of a fly's wings may happen too quickly to be captured by a 25 frames-per-second video camera, but most things happening on human-perceptible time frames during a movie are slow by comparison. Even the most action-packed chase scenes are pretty boring if taken slowly, frame-by-frame, one at a time.

Imagine James Bond flying down the alleyways of an exotic city at 150 mph in a European sports car. That is a pretty intense scene, but even during this scene, very little changes in the twenty-fifth of a second that passes between each frame. In fact, most of the frame stays exactly the same much of the time. So, in order to save space, the software throws away everything that did not change. After all, if little is changing, why save the same frame twice?

Instead of saving every frame, the MPEG-4 format, the video equivalent of MP3 audio, just takes one frame every second or so, also known as the key frame. Until the next key frame arrives, no other frames are stored. Instead, only the parts of the frame that have changed are stored. So, if James Bond is flying down the city street, instead of storing the picture of the street over and over again and wasting huge amounts of disc space, the lossy MPEG software will just say, "Move the image of the street a little bit to the left." The technical details of how it accomplishes these feats are enough to drive even mathematicians crazy, but as a podcaster, you do not need to worry about these details.

If that is the case, you might be asking yourself: Why does this matter to an aspiring podcaster? It matters a great deal. Lossy compression is great, but once this information is thrown out, it never comes back again, and this has two major consequences.

The first is that it is possible to get too greedy. The software will let you throw away as much information as you want, to the point of turning your podcast into an unbearable mess of static

and distortion. It will take some skill to find the perfect settings to balance disk space requirements with quality control. On the audio side, you can push your audio to the point that it sounds less like a high-fidelity CD and more like a distant (and fading) AM radio station playing on a $5 radio. On the video side, images become increasingly grainy and distorted and motions begin to stutter.

Second, and more importantly, you might be able to throw the info out once, but that is about it. If you decide to distribute your podcast in the MP3 format, and a year down the road decide to switch to some new audio format that is taking the podcasting world by storm, you are going to see a substantial drop in quality when converting the original MP3 file to the new format.

It is a bit like the children's game "telephone." Standing in a line, children pass a message from the beginning of the line to the end of the line, and usually, by the time the message reaches the end of the line, the message has been hopelessly garbled by the accumulative mistakes of dozens of voices and ears, often with quite humorous results. This was demonstrated by magician Mac King in a Las Vegas show once. The message "Mac King is a comedy magic genius" was, after being whispered around a room filled with over 600 people, transformed into "Macaroni cantaloupe knows the future." With lossy compression, this problem is much worse because with each run through the compressor, the software is deliberately throwing away some of the information it received. Like a game of "telephone," the translation is accurate only the first few times, and then becomes increasingly garbled, until only static remains.

How a Computer Measures Disc Space

One constant source of confusion, even among those familiar with computers, is the way computers measure the size of a file. At its most basic form, computers use two different terms to measure space: bits and bytes, which are measured like this:

1 byte = 8 bits

It does not help the confusion that the two words both begin with a 'b' and are not used with a great deal of consistency. File sizes and download speeds are usually described in bytes, but Internet speeds and measurements of file quality are usually described in terms of the smaller bit. This book will spell out, each time a term is used, whether it is referring to bits or bytes.

Because each measurement is so small — a byte is only large enough to hold about one letter in an ordinary text document — a number of larger terms are also used to describe them. For esoteric technical reasons, even these conversions can get confusing; it is a common mistake to think that each prefix represents an increase of 1,000. However, they actually break down as follows:

1 kilobyte = 1024 bytes

1 megabyte = 1024 kilobytes

1 gigabyte = 1024 megabytes

1 terabyte = 1024 gigabytes

File Quality

The maximum quality for audio and video recordings stored on a computer are described using two measurements: bit rates and sample rates. The bit rate of your audio file is a number that describes how much space will be used, in bits, by every second of your podcast. Most of the time, computer users measure space used on their computers in bytes, but a bit is a little different. A bit is a computer term that describes the smallest possible piece of information storable on a computer. There are eight bits in one byte. An example of a low-quality audio file, comparable to the quality of an AM radio, would be a 32–kilobits-per-second (kbps) MP3 file. Because there are eight bits in each byte and 1024 bits in a kilobit, this means the resulting audio file will take up four kilobytes of disc space every second, or about one megabyte every four minutes.

At the other extreme, a 320-kbps MP3 file has quality that rivals even high-fidelity compact discs. Quality comes at a cost though, as the 320 kbps bit rate MP3 takes up to ten times as much as much space as its 32 kbps counterpart. Instead of each megabyte holding four minutes, each megabyte will hold only 24 seconds of audio. In short, higher audio quality means larger podcast MP3 files, and that means longer download times for your listeners and potentially higher bandwidth fees from your Web host. *How to set the bit rate will be discussed in Chapter 6 on post-production, as well as which factors will affect your decision.*

Variable bit rate

Variable bit rate (VBR) is a technology that allows an MP3 to vary the bit rate in mid-recording. The codec, or the software used to create the MP3 file, will reduce the bit rate during simplistic areas of the recording and increase it again during the more detailed areas of the recording. This can be a useful tool for saving space while still assuring that the full quality is there when needed. There are a few disadvantages to using a VBR file to hold your recording. The most important is that not all media players support variable bit rates. If you choose to distribute your show in a

VBR format, any listener who attempts to play back your podcast on a device that does not support it will get a jumbled mess of a recording. New MP3 players should work without problem, but some older ones might have little or buggy VBR support. Another disadvantage is that VBR files are more complex than those that do not use the technology, and it will take a longer time for the computer to create the file for distribution at the end of the post-production phase.

Sample rate

Whereas the bit rate tries to describe the quality of sound in terms of the amount of space that will be used to store it, with more space equaling a higher-quality sound, the sample rate looks at it from another angle. The sample rate measures the number of times, per second, the volume of the sound will be written to the disc, and it will have a heavy emphasis on the range of frequencies, from high-pitch to low-pitch, that your podcast will be able to play back to the listener. To give a sense of context, an audio CD usually has a sample rate of 44 kHz, and the vast majority of people are happy with that. However, some audiophiles with especially sensitive ears and great sound systems insist that they can hear the difference in quality between 44 kHz and higher sample rates. For a voice-only podcast, you can get away with as little as 8 kHz, but it is better to play it safe and go for a sample rate of at least 22 kHz, if not the full, CD-quality 44 kHz. Higher settings are possible but unnecessary for even the most discerning of podcasts.

A final note is that this refers to the maximum quality available. If the source recording is of poor quality, no increase in bit rate or sample rate will improve it. Indeed, increasing the bit rate and

sample rate above the values that were used in the recording achieves nothing, and only wastes disc space as the computer sets aside file space to hold information it does not possess.

ID3 tags

ID3 tags are small pieces of information attached to audio files that tell the listener important information about the audio files, such as the artist, publisher, and title. Most MP3 players and media software are able to read this information from the file and allow the listener to see the artist and song name while they are listening. Both Audacity and GarageBand, which are covered in the next two chapters, support writing information to ID3 tags.

The Lossless formats

There are three lossless formats in regular use. None of these are used to distribute podcasts: each consumes far too much space per minute of quality audio for this purpose, but they are excellent candidates for master copies, since they preserve all the information recorded exactly as it was received.

WAV

WAV stands for the Waveform Audio File Format. It was developed by IBM and Microsoft to store uncompressed audio. Encoding methods can vary greatly within the WAV format, but the essential trait to remember is that nearly all systems support it, and it consumes massive amounts of space for CD-quality audio.

AIFF

AIFF stands for Audio Interchange File Format, but you might want to substitute the "Audio" for "Apple." It is essentially the Apple Macintosh version of Microsoft's WAV format. It is not as widely supported as WAV, but most major programs will support it.

WMA

WMA stands for Windows Media Audio. It is Microsoft's intended replacement for the older WAV format and supports both lossless and lossy versions. It is not as widely supported as either WAV or AIFF, however. In fact, few programs outside the Windows operating system can use it reliably.

The lossy formats

There are four lossy formats in common use, and nearly all podcasts are distributed using one of these formats. They save huge amounts of space at a small cost in sound quality.

MP3

MP3 stands for MPEG 1 Audio Layer 3. It was developed by the Moving Picture Experts Group (MPEG) as a tool for storing sound tracks for movies on video CDs and DVDs. It is the most widely used and widely supported of all the lossy formats.

- AAC

AAC stands for Advanced Audio Coding is the planned successor to MP3 and generally offers better quality at lower bit-rates. Though it is unquestionably superior to MP3, some older devices do not support AAC.

Ogg Vorbis

Both MP3 and AAC are patented technologies, which require licensing fees to use in a product. In response to this, the open-source community has created Ogg Vorbis, an audio format similar to MP3 and AAC, but free for anyone that wants to use it. However, it is not generally supported by portable media devices like the iPod.

WMA

Unlike many of the formats here, Microsoft's WMA has both a lossy and lossless version, each with the same advantages and disadvantages.

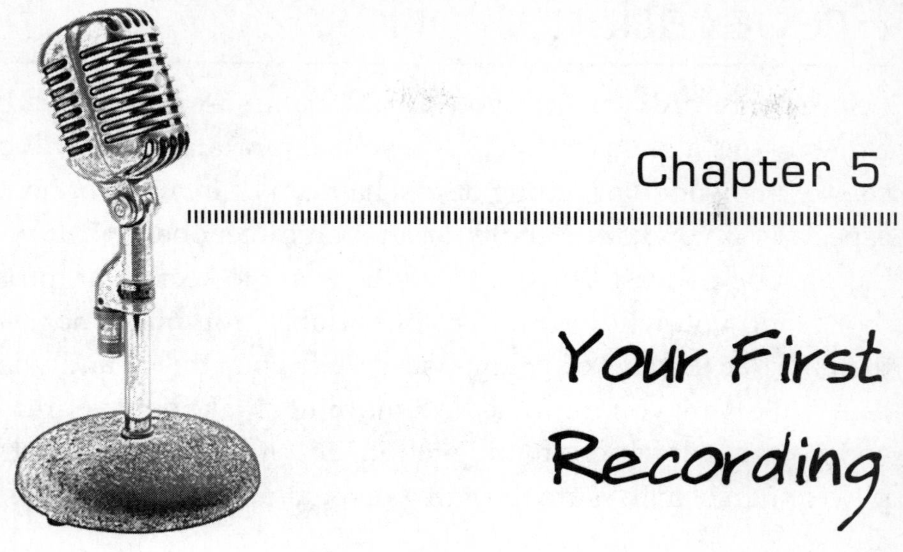

Chapter 5

Your First Recording

Now that you have gotten an idea of what hardware and software you might be working with, it is time to take a test run and see how a basic recording session might go, using two programs: GarageBand for Mac OS X and Audacity for Windows, Linux, and Mac OS X. GarageBand is part of Apple's iLife suite, which will cost you about $40, but it also comes standard with all new Apple computers, so you might already have a copy of it. Audacity, on the other hand, is free, and although its user interface is a little more primitive than its Apple-made cousin, it has a similar mix of features. So get ready. The moment is here. It is time to hit that big red button and see how you sound.

Preparation Work

Before the recording starts, you should make sure you are ready. Do you have a glass of water? Are you comfortable? You will be shocked how loud a shifting office chair can be in a microphone, especially if you had to settle for an omnidirectional one. If you have a long podcast, you will need the water to keep your throat moist, and you will want to be comfortable. You might not feel the effect at the end of your podcast, but your throat and your back will thank you for it the next morning. Make sure your mic and your headphones are plugged in, and if they need an extra power source, make sure they are powered up.

Crank the volume, close your eyes, and listen for any preventable noise through your headpones. This could be anything from fans to the sound of distant traffic floating through the open window. If you hear noises, do something about it. Sometimes you just have to make do, but often a better quality sound requires nothing more than closing a door elsewhere in your home. If you have a script, get it ready and in a place where you can comfortably read it.

How to Speak into a Microphone

There is an art to speaking into the microphone, and each microphone will handle differently. You want to stay far enough away from the microphone that it will not amplify the air leaving your mouth, particularly when you use plosive sounds like "B" and "P" because these produce a distracting "pop" sound. However, you want to be close enough to utilize the proximity effect, which is the tendency of a microphone to deepen the sound of a person's voice when he or she gets closer to it. It is a very pleasant sounding effect, for both male and female voices.

Many professional recording studios take this a step further and eliminate the chair, especially if particularly creative vocal work is needed. If your goal is a 1940s-era radio show, you may want to follow this step as well. Body posture can have a pretty profound effect on the sound of a person's voice, especially if portraying a character that is performing some physical action. However, few podcasters go to this extreme, and most succeed in bringing out all the emotive power they need while sitting in a comfortable chair.

Handheld microphones

Most people have an instinctive sense of how to hold a simple, handheld dynamic microphone. The top of the microphone should face directly toward the mouth of the speaker. There are only two common mistakes. The first is to hold the mic either too close or too far away from the mouth. If you have chosen a handheld microphone, then the best way to get a feel for it is experimentation. Experiment with different distances until you find one a pleasant one.

The second is harder to avoid. New podcasters using handheld microphones will acquire a good sense of how to hold the microphone early on but forget about microphone position later in the show. Because the mind is justifiably thinking about multiple things during a show, it is easy to forget the little things. As this happens, the podcaster moves the microphone around restlessly and tilts it away from his or her mouth as he or she forgets about it. The result is constant variations in loudness and pitch.

For this reason, it may be good to invest in a cheap microphone stand, so you can keep your mind on the show instead of the position of the mic.

Recording

The long wait is over. If you are using Mac OS X and have a copy of iLife, you ought to go to the GarageBand section and follow that tutorial. Otherwise, or if you simply prefer to learn another program, read on about Audacity, the open-source audio suite. Free versions are available for Windows, Macs, and Linux machines on the Audacity Web page at **http://audacity.sourceforge.net**.

Audacity

Recording for the first time in Audacity, you will be greeted with an introduction window.

Before going any further, you need to configure the settings in Audacity. Click "File" and then "Preferences." You will be confronted with a lot of information that you probably will not understand yet, but that is OK. Click the "Recording" tab and turn on "Software Play-through." This allows you to listen to yourself on headphones while you record, and this is always the best practice because it allows you to spot mistakes early on.

You might see another option for "Sound Activated Recording," depending on your version of Audacity. It is a twist on the "gate" tool. In theory, gates ignore all sound below a certain minimum volume to lower the amount of ambient noise that actually makes it through to the recording. Used with a soft touch in an already reasonably quiet environment, a gate can give pauses the depth of silence they deserve. However, if an environment is noisy even in the slightest, a gate can make the quality of a recording much worse when ambient noise comes screaming in every time the host speaks. For now, leave "Sound Activated Recording" turned off, because one thing you want to do during this first recording is get a good sense of your noise floor, or how much ambient noise remains after your best efforts to eliminate it, and you do not want a gate canceling any of it out just yet. Try enabling Sound Activated Recording later to see whether you like the results.

Next, click the Quality tab. Ensure that your sample rate is at least 44 kHz and that you are recording with "32-bit float" or "24-bit" format. If you use 16-bit, you will probably not get the dynamic range you need, especially for a master copy.

Click the "Directories" tab. You will see an option for playing from and recording to RAM. If you have the memory for it, recording to RAM can make your recording and editing work go much faster because the audio work is being done in the fast RAM memory and not off the slower hard drive. It is not a good idea to try this with less than two gigabytes of RAM, however.

Close the "Preferences" window and hit the big red "Record" button. Say a few things and adjust the volume on your headphones so your voice sounds the same coming through the headphones as it does inside your head. You will also want to adjust your distance relative to the microphone. Try to get as close to the microphone as you can while speaking in a normal tone and without producing audible rushes of wind or popping sounds with plosives. As you speak, watch the level meters in the top right portion of your window. There is a lot to keep balanced. Do not get frustrated because it takes some time to get it just right. Time spent getting a feel for your microphone and getting your levels straightened out pays dividends in the quality of your podcast. Repeat this procedure quickly each time you begin your podcast to ensure the levels are right and that there is no preventable background noise. Just do it at the beginning of every recording and remove the time spent on setup and testing later in post-production.

The left meter, in green, measures the sound being output to the speakers or headphones. The right meter, in red, measures the sound coming in from the microphone.

The purple bars in each image record the peak, or highest volume level, for the entire recording, and the thin colored bars measure the peak for the last few seconds. As a rule of thumb, the meter should never max out. In fact, if it does at any point during the recording, it will show a bright red bar at the end of the meter to indicate that an overload has happened. In post-production, you will be able to apply the "compressor" effect to try to repair a little of the damage, but it is always best, if you notice the overload when it happens, to do a second take immediately when possible.

Speaking in a normal tone should only keep each meter between ¼ and ½ full. This gives you plenty of room to raise or lower your voice without overloading the range.

Adjust the volume for your microphone so that when you are speaking in a normal tone of voice the bars remain comfortably in the bottom half to center of the range. Raise your voice a bit to ensure that, even when speaking loudly, the range remains below ¾ of the bar.

Because this is a test recording, go ahead and crank the microphone volume all the way to the maximum value, and say a few things to see if you can drive the level meter into overdrive. This occurs when you get the red warning bar at the end of the meter.

Hit the stop button and listen to your recording. Turn up the volume a bit on your headphones and make a note of any noise you hear in the background. When you reach the section where you overloaded the file, you will hear that your voice gains a metallic, distorted sound, and the further you went over the bar, the greater the distortion will be.

Click "File" and "Save Project." Name it "My First Recording Raw." This creates a project file for Audacity, which you can open and edit later. It takes up a great deal of space (about ten megabytes per minute), but it will be saved in a lossless state that ensures you always have a pristine copy to work from. Remember, you can divide audio formats into two groups: lossy and lossless. Lossy formats, like MP3, save a great deal of space, but throw large amounts of audio data in the trash in the process. Doing this once or twice is too little for most listeners to notice, which is why you can distribute your podcast as an MP3. However, repeated changes to an MP3 file can degrade the quality quickly, and you always want to have something pristine around you can work from, saved in one of the lossless formats, like WAV or AIFF.

Before post-production, you should do one last thing. Click "File" and "Save Project As." Name this new copy "My First Recording Master," so you can keep the original recording separate from any work you do in post-production. That way, if you apply a filter in post-production, save your work, and come back the next day, you can still go back to the original, raw recording if a fresh listen reveals that the effect was not as good as you thought it was.

With a little luck, the overload is salvageable. Go to the main menu, click "Effect," and select "Compressor." You will be given a window with a lot of sliders and a graph. *In Chapter 6, you will learn a bit about how to customize the compressor to your needs.* But for now, the default options are fine. Click "OK" and wait for it to finish. If you watch carefully, you will notice the waveforms in the track window shrink, especially in the area where you overloaded the track. The compressor succeeded in removing the distortion, but you should not count on the software compressor. It is better that the overload never happens rather than crossing your fingers and hoping Audacity can fix your mistake.

Finally, click "File" again and choose "Export." This creates a compressed version of your recording that you can distribute. Audacity provides a very powerful interface for controlling every detail of your distributed file. *This will be discussed further in Chapter 6 on post-production.* For now, just choose "MP3 Files" and click "Save."

Congratulations! You have successfully done your first recording, put it through some rudimentary post-production, and created an MP3 file that listeners can play in their MP3 players. It is not a podcast yet without a server and an RSS file, but the hardest work is done.

GarageBand

For Mac users, it is time to take your first test run with GarageBand. After starting GarageBand, you will immediately be presented with a window that asks you whether you would like to create a new project or create a new podcast episode. Both of these options are virtually the same, but creating the podcast episode will start you off with a few podcasting settings turned on, so choose this option and name the project "My first recording."

After starting, you will be presented with the basic user interface. On the right is your media browser. Photos from iPhoto®; movies from iMovie®, iPhoto®, Photo Booth®, or iTunes®; and audio from iTunes and other GarageBand projects can be dragged into your podcast to add multimedia effects to your podcast. However, for now you should keep it simple. Click the glowing blue media button to close your media tray.

You will notice four tracks already in your podcast: the podcast track, which holds your artwork, a track each for a male and a female host, and a "jingles" track to play back music during your show. You can add and remove tracks later by using the plus button.

At the bottom of the screen is your track editor, and it will change depending upon the type of track you have selected.

Now, select the "male voice" or "female voice" track and click the information button to open the track information table on the right side of the screen.

Next to the option that says monitor, select "On." If you do not have your headphones on, put them on. You should now be able to hear your own voice coming back to you when you speak.

Another option you will see under the monitor menu is "On with Feedback Protection." Feedback is an electrical phenomenon that occurs when a microphone picks up the sound of its own recording coming out of a speaker. You have probably heard it before at a concert or some other live performance where microphones were used to amplify a speaker or band. The closest comparison one could make is to imagine the sound of a giant hand scratching a giant chalkboard. It is unpleasant, to say the least, and it is the last thing you want in your podcast. Feedback protection is an optional feature that will mute the microphone if any feedback is detected. However, GarageBand's Feedback Protection option is slightly paranoid. Feedback is a serious problem, but having a recording session dramatically interrupted, sometimes mid-sentence, by the Feedback Protection option is not, in practice, a good solution. Because you are using headphones and not speakers, it would be better to leave it turned off.

Say a few things and watch the volume meter for your track, the green bars, as you do so. The green bars represent your current volume and the single green line represents the peak you have reached in the last few seconds.

With a normal tone, the green bars should never exceed the halfway point on the track. If the green bars are barely moving at all, increase the recording level in the information panel just a notch until they hover around the ¼ mark.

Raise your voice. The green bars should not go past ¾ of the meter. If the red lights on the right go on, your recording level is too high. Turn it down a bit. Whenever the bars are in the red, you have exceeded the dynamic range of the audio file and your recording is being distorted and filled with static.

Do not get frustrated if it takes some careful adjusting to get it right. Eventually, you will find a sweet spot from which you can alter your tone of voice naturally. Once you have found it, change your focus to volume. Adjust the volume until the sound of your voice coming to you from the headphones roughly equals the sound of your voice as you hear it in your head.

Before you record anything, sit quietly for a moment and listen for noise. Can you hear traffic outside, people elsewhere in the house, pets, ceiling fans, or the air conditioner? Try to eliminate any of this noise if you can. Close windows and doors. Lead pets to a more distant part of the house. Close air vents and turn off fans.

Shift your weight in your seat and listen for the creaking sound of the chair. Click a few times with your mouse. Type a little bit on the keyboard. Try to get a clear impression of how loudly different actions in your studio space are going to appear on the microphone. If the sound of your mouse is unnecessarily loud, try to move it further away from your microphone. If you have a reclining chair, and the sound of it shifting appears on the microphone, lock it during recording. Turn away from the microphone and take a sip of water. Can you hear yourself slurping the water? If so, turn the microphone down because you will probably need water during your podcast.

Time to record! Ensure the male or female track is still selected and hit the record button. The track will slowly begin to fill with a red bar. In the track editor at the bottom of the screen, you will see a rough outline of the waveform being recorded. Say a few things into the microphone and watch the recording.

Toward the end of your recording, open the information panel again and make a note of your recording level and push it up to the max to see if you can drive the recording into overdrive.

When you have finished, hit the record button again to stop. Go to the "File" menu and choose "Save."

You have finished your first recording. Go back to the beginning and click the 00:00 in the timeline. Click the play button and listen to the entire recording. Listen for noise and any other distractions. When you reach the overloaded part, notice how your voice sounds metallic. Now it is time for post-production.

Open the information panel and click the arrow next to "Details." A list of effects open with some of them already turned on. Turn on the "Compressor" effect and, from the list of presets, choose the "Limiter Hard" option. Find the loudest part in your recording, and click the timeline just to the left of it and hit play. This should remove some of the distortion.

Unlike Audacity, GarageBand projects always maintain a pristine copy of the original recording without effects, and then applies the effects to that recording as needed, so there is no need to store a separate "raw" copy of your recordings. If you do not like a given effect, it can always be adjusted or turned off later.

Now that you have finished your first effort at post-production, click "Share" and "Export Song to Disc." You are given three choices. First, you could disable compression, save, and export a full-quality version of the recording. Alternatively, you can use either the AAC or MP3 as a file format. Choose MP3 and go with the "High Quality" option. *Chapter 6 will go into more detail about the differences between MP3 and AAC and the features available in the "Custom" options for each format.*

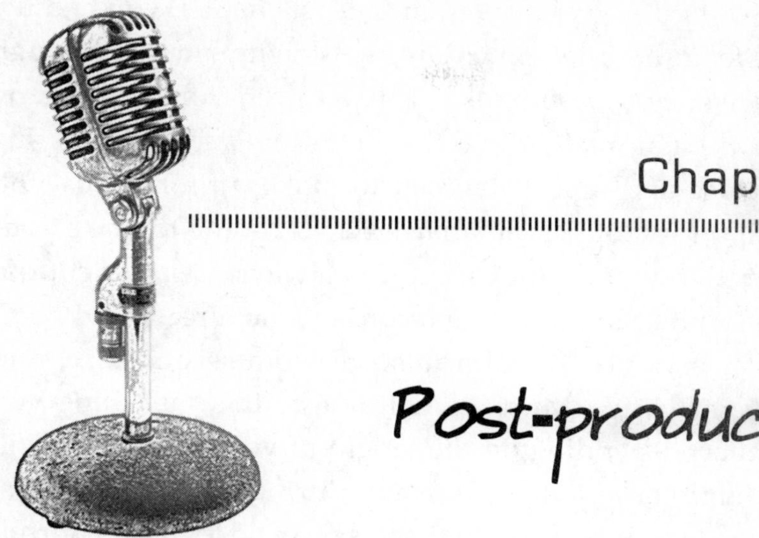

Chapter 6

Post-production

You have finished your first recording, but there are probably a few rough edges that need sanded down and polished. How you do this is going to depend partially on which program you use. Both Audacity and GarageBand are covered here, and between the two of them, you should know enough to transfer the concepts to other programs.

GarageBand

Shortcuts

SPACE BAR . . . . . . Play

BACKSPACE . . . . . Delete Selection

Cmd-Z (Windows-Z) . . Undo Last Action

Cmd-Shift-K" . . . . . . Open Musical Typing.

If you followed the advice given in the last chapter, you had the "Monitor" feature turned on and were listening intently through your headphones as you spoke. This allowed you to hear any ambient noise that made it into the recording, such as a passing car, and pause and repeat yourself to make up for it. Just following that one bit of preventative advice is going to make your post-production work a lot easier. It is always easier to cut out mistakes that you caught during recording and already did a second take on than it is to cut a mistake, do a second take, and make it all match up. Mistakes will not be the only thing you remove either; depending on the length of your show, you will almost certainly need a drink of water during the recording session. Your podcast is not live, so there is no need to make yourself uncomfortable. However, sips of water or other distractions tend to produce unnatural pauses and dead air, and you will want to remove those before the episode goes online.

If you do not already have your project opened in GarageBand, open it up. The first thing you want to do is select the track you recorded to "male voice" or "female voice," and click the scissors button to open your detailed editor pane at the bottom of the page. This will show you a detailed waveform, a series of squiggly lines representing the sound of your voice. The larger the squiggle, the louder the sound. There will also be a small slider bar at the bottom left of the editor pane, and this changes the zoom on the waveform. Adjust the slider bar until you can clearly make out the difference between words and silence in the waveform. This might take some experimentation. If you want to check a specific area of the waveform, you can click and drag over that portion with your left mouse button in the waveform view. After you finish, press the space bar, and it will play that portion of your audio. You can also press the Play button, which

looks like an arrow, but you will find the short cuts faster. You can reference the short cut list at the top of this section whenever you need help. You can also click "Help" and "Keyboard Shortcuts" to get a list of all the short cuts.

Removing a section

Listen to your podcast episode. Notice that a red line will follow the current recording in both the top, track-based view and the bottom, waveform view. Wait until you hear a mistake or an absurdly long pause, and hit the space bar (or the pause button) to stop at that point, so you can remove it. If your first recording was perfect, find a spot to remove for practice (but be sure to click "Edit," "Undo" at the end to restore your pristine audio).

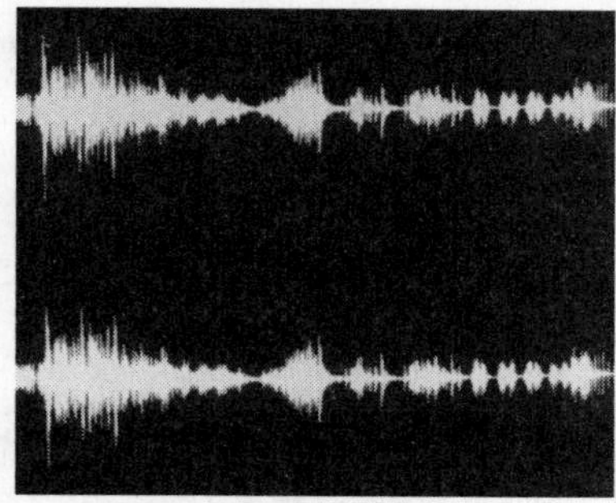

Audio waveform

In the waveform view, left-click and drag over the mistake portion to highlight it. You can press the space bar to test the highlighted portion to see if it is large enough. If you are confident that it is, single-click it with your mouse. It will instantly be highlight in purple, and you will be able to see the upper view that it has been cut off from the rest of the audio. Press the backspace key to delete it. It will be replaced with a completely blank space.

Leave the waveform view and go up to the track based view at the top of the screen. Your audio is now divided into two parts. Hold down the mouse button over the right-hand part to select it. So long as you are holding the mouse button down, you can drag that portion of the audio anywhere you like. Pull it with the mouse so that it matches up precisely with the end of the previous section, but make sure they do not overlap. Press "space" again to play and ensure that everything sounds okay now that your mistake has been removed. It might take some experimentation to get the two sections situated so that the pause between them sounds natural. Finally, merge the two sections back together again. To do this, hold down the Cmd button (or "Windows" button on a Microsoft keyboard), and click each section once with the mouse to highlight them both. Release the Cmd button, and then press "Cmd-J." Alternatively, you can use the menu option "Tools," "Join" after you have selected each section.

If you only doing this for practice and do not really want to remove a portion of your recording, now is a good time to click "Edit" and "Undo." You might need to repeat this three or four times, as the steps you followed are undone, one at a time. You can also press "Cmd-z" on your keyboard for the same effect.

Other options in the waveform editor

There are three other options in the waveform editor. They are rarely used by podcasters, but you should know about their existence. The first is the "Pitch." By adjusting this slider from its default value of zero, you can adjust the pitch of the audio in the recording. For example, a setting of "5" raises the pitch and produces an effect very similar to the effect of breathing in the air from a helium balloon or the music of the parody band "Alvin and the Chipmunks." Alternatively, a setting of "-5" produces a far deeper sound, similar to how a demon might sound in a horror movie.

The other two are "Enhanced Tuning" and "Enhanced Timing." If you cannot see these options, click the small grey arrow next to the word "Region" in the wave editor. These options are rarely used for ordinary spoken podcasts. Instead, they are designed for singers and instrumental tracks. The first forces the pitch of the sounds to conform to the nearest pitch on a musical staff, while the second forces the lengths of sounds to conform to a certain length of note (from quarter notes to sixteenth notes.) If you plan on recording live music for your podcast, these can be useful features for enhancing the quality of the music.

Adding jingles

Click the eye icon to close the WavefForm Editor and open the jingles selector. GarageBand comes with a respectable library of short instrumentals, all free to use in your projects without royalty or copyright concerns. At first, the jingles editor can be a little overwhelming, so let's go quickly over the basic fundamentals of how it works. At the bottom left are a panel of view selection buttons. One looks like a window, the next like a musical note, and the last like an antenna. Click the "window" button. This allows you to select a jingle by genre, mood, or instrument using a view similar to the multi-column view in Finder. Next, click the musical note button. This gives you a list of instruments, moods, and genres all together in a grid. By clicking one of the buttons, you can restrict the list to only jingles that fit that description. One of the best features of this view is the ability to combine multiple qualifiers. For example, if you want to see only electric guitars playing rock music with a relaxed mood, then you would click the buttons "Electric," "Guitar," "Rock," and "Relaxed." If you decide you would rather try an acoustic guitar, you can click electric again to deselect it and click "acoustic." This can be a powerful way to browse the library of hundreds of jingles. Finally, click the "antenna" icon. This sorts the library into a selection of jingles, stingers, and sound effects. It also allows you to filter jingles based on whether they fit into a "major" or "minor" scale. With the exception of the side effects (which are only visible in the antenna view), all the jingles are the same in each view; the only difference is how you prefer to access them.

Select a jingle you like and drag it with your mouse to "jingles" track in the top of the program. Press the "spacebar" to start playing, and now you can hear the music at the start of your podcast. Go to the 'Male Voice' (or "Female Voice") track and drag it with the left mouse button a little to the right to ensure that the music plays for a second or two before you start talking. Use the timer meter at the very top of the program to guide you.

This sounds pretty good, as it is, but the music should fade out as the voice comes in. On the "jingles" track, click the big black down arrow to open the track options bar. This will add a solid blue line to the track view. Ensure that the option listed says "Track Volume." Find the spot on the track volume for the jingles located just a few seconds before your vocal track begins on the male or female vocal line. Click that spot on the line and a blue bubble will appear. This will mark the beginning of the fade. Now go to a few seconds after you have begun to speak and click the line again. Another bubble will appear, and it will mark the end of the fade. Now, drag this bubble down to the bottom of the track. Hit the space bar to test it out; your jingle should now play for a few seconds before you being to talk and slowly start to fade out.

Now, go to the end of your track, and repeat the same steps at the end: drag a jingle to the end of the position, so that it ends a few seconds after your vocals end. Click on the track-volume bar to produce two bubbles: one to indicate the start of your jingles fade in and another to indicate the end of it. Drag the end marker up until the readout says "0 db," which means no amplification and no fade. This allows your jingle to begin playing louder and louder as your show ends. Click a location on the time line at the top of the screen just before your jingle begins, and click play to hear what it sounds like.

Finally, click "Track" and "Fade Out" to have everything on the show fade out at the end of the show.

You now have your show starting with a jingle, which fades out smoothly into your voice. Then, at the end of the show, the jingle slowly fades back in over your voice. Finally, the jingle itself fades out. Pretty snappy, but you do not need to depend on the jingles provided by GarageBand. If you have the ability, GarageBand is a powerful tool for creating your own.

Writing your own jingles

Press the "+" button to create a new track on your podcast. You will be given a choice between the two track types: the software instrument track and the real instrument track. So far, you have used only "real instrument" tracks: tracks designed to play recordings of sounds coming from a microphone or some other real instrument. However, you are not restricted to these; you can also produce your own jingles using a software instrument. This uses a special music format called the Musical Instrument Digital Interface (MIDI) to store sounds. Instead of recording the sound itself, MIDI stores a musical notation of the sound to be reproduced later with sound hardware. Select "Software Instrument Track."

A new track is created named "Grand Piano" with a picture of a grand piano as its avatar. Click the small headphones button on that track. This will 'solo' it, or make it so you can hear only sounds from that track during playback. You could also click the speaker icon on all the other tracks to mute them one by one.

Click the "i" button for the information panel. Notice that it has changed; rather than a list of effects, you are given a list of hundreds of instruments, from pianos to guitars, drums, and even special effects like applause and laughter. Choose guitars and "Big Electric Lead."

Now, you have two choices for how to enter the music for your new jingle. If you own a keyboard that supports MIDI, you can play practically any instrument in GarageBand, and record the results, by playing your keyboard. However, MIDI keyboards can be expensive, and for the rest of us, GarageBand includes a feature called "musical typing." Click "Window" and "Musical Typing." Alternatively, you can press Cmd-Shift-K. This opens a small piano keyboard on your screen notated according to the keys on your ordinary computer keyboard. For example, Press the record button and, one at a time, press the following keys to play a simple scale: A S D F G (pause) H G F D S. Then press stop. You can now play it back.

Also, if you click the "scissors" icon, you can see that the familiar waveform view has been replaced with two versions of musical notation. One indicates the position of the notes with solid bars while the other renders the music you just played into classical musical notation. In both views, you can move the notes around on the staff as needed to correct mistakes or rework it into new compositions simply by clicking and dragging with your mouse.

This takes a great deal of practice, and musical theory and composition are well beyond the scope of this book, but the tools are there.

Sound enhancement presets

GarageBand comes with a pretty nifty suite of sound enhancement options for your perusal. Close the jingles box by clicking the eye button and then the "i" button. Click the "male" or "female" voice track, as appropriate. You should already be familiar with the "Monitor" option from the last chapter, which reroutes the recording sound back to your headphones, but there are a huge number of other options lurking underneath the "details" tab. Click it, and let's explore some of the advanced features of GarageBand.

You will be given a long list of options (some of them with mystifying names like "AURogerBeep"). But you will also have a list of easy to understand "presets" with much easier names like "Male Narrator" and "Male Narrator Noisy." Select one of them and hit the spacebar to hear the difference it makes. Each time you change your preset, you will notice multiple changes happening in the details section. For example, "Male Narrator Noisy" turns on the "Speech Enhancer" and adds a small amount of bass reduction to the recording, while "Female Radio" adds some reverb, a very, very slight echo, to the recording. There are even presets that attempts to turn vocals into different instruments. Feel free to experiment with the different presets, but ultimately, you will find yourself coming back to Male and Female Narrator and, in a noisy environment, Male and Female Narrator Noise. These find a good balance of sound enhancements for most of the situations you will find yourself in as a podcaster. However, if you feel like getting fancy, the following sections detail the most common settings. *There are dozens of others, and those are covered briefly in the guide to GarageBand sound enhancements in Appendix D.*

Compressor

The compressor in GarageBand restricts the dynamic range, or the difference between the loudest and quietest parts of the recording, by reducing the volume of the loudest portions of the audio: those over its "threshold" setting. The most common use of a compressor is to increase the volume of an entire show without risking the distortion that would occur if a particularly loud portion overwhelmed the dynamic range, or the volume limits, of a speaker.

GarageBand comes with a number of compressor presets for likely recording situations. However, you can also adjust the threshold, ration, attack, and gain settings yourself. The threshold is how loud the audio is allowed to get before further increases in volume are scaled down. The threshold is not a volume limit. It is possible for audio to exceed the threshold value. Imagine an audio signal that comes into the microphone at 100 dB with a threshold of 50. Instead of being reduced to 50, it will be reduced to a value between 50 and 100. The precise value is determined by the ratio. This determines how quickly volume levels above the threshold are allowed to rise. The higher the ratio, the harder sounds are pushed down to the threshold. The attack determines how quickly the compressor takes effect; with a fast attack, the compressor kicks in immediately after the sound rises above the threshold, whereas a slow attack makes the process smoother. Finally, the gain allows you to boost the volume of the entire audio track by a single, preset amount.

The presets should work with most common podcasting situations, but feel free to experiment with the various settings looking for the best overall sound. Changes to the compressor settings, like all changes to GarageBand's post-production settings, do not become permanent until the results are exported to disk. Even then, you can always reopen the master recording and create a new export.

Speech enhancer

The speech enhancer setting actually combines a number of other plugins in a single, easy-to-use interface. Each of the presets in the in the GarageBand podcasting category actually refer to the various settings of the speech enhancer plugin. The plugin attempts to reduce ambient noise, emphasize key frequencies for either male or female voices, and apply a variety of other subtle effects, depending on the precise model of microphone used. Settings are included for the built-in mikes of every recent model of Apple computer. It is a good idea to always have the speech enhancer turned on, unless you have a concrete reason for turning it off.

Gate

The gate attempts to reduce ambient noise by automatically turning off the microphone during periods of silence and turning it back on again during periods of sound. Used subtly, it can make a quiet environment even quieter, but when it is over used or used in an already loud environment, the result is unpleasant and results in deep silences punctuated by a rush of ambient noise every time the host speaks. This is because the gate does not actually try to remove the noise; it only cuts the microphone on and off depending on the volume of the sound coming from the microphone.

You can even use the sound enhancement features for software instrument tracks like the one you made in the section on making your own jingles. They are all post-production effects. You can add or remove them as you like after a recording. Feel free to experiment, as none of these settings alter the source audio and are not made permanent until you export to disk.

Setting the metadata

Metadata is the extra information built into each episode of your podcast that provides information about it. Later, it will be integrated into your RSS feed, which is described in Chapter 8, but GarageBand allows you to add the information now so supporting programs can put it in your RSS feed automatically. With the "i" pane still open, click the track that says "Podcast Track." All of the options previously filling the right side of the screen will disappear and be replaced by six options: an artwork bar, a title, the artist and composer, the iTunes parental advisory rating, and a description. Your parental advisory ratings have only two options: clean and explicit. *These options are covered in greater detail in the iTunes section of Chapter 8.* You can add a logo to your podcast easily; simply drag an image file into the image box, which, by default, will read "No Artwork Available." You can also click the media button, which is located next to the "i" button, and drag any pictures from iPhoto or Photo Booth directly onto the Podcast track, which, be default, will read "Drag Artwork Here," helpfully enough.

Exporting to disk

Click "Share" and "Export Song to Disk." You have a choice between exporting it as an uncompressed file, which will be many hundreds of megabytes in size, or a compressed one. Select "Compressed." You will have two options: to use the AAC format or the MP3 format. AAC is generally better than MP3, offering higher quality at lower bitrates and file sizes. In fact, it was designed specifically to replace the MP3 format, but it is not yet as widely supported as MP3. So, for now, choose MP3. You will be given a choice between three quality settings: good, high, and highest. Good is acceptable for voice, but podcasts in which music is a primary focus (not counting jingles), should go for either high or highest settings. Alternatively, you can select "custom" and specify the precise settings to be used by the encoder, including the exact bit rate, whether to use "Variable Bit Rate" encoding to have the computer guess automatically which parts of the show need more quality and which need less, and even specify whether to export in stereo or mono. Two settings you might find mysterious however are "Joint Stereo" and "Filter Frequencies Below 10 Hz."

Joint Stereo attempts to save space by recording only one channel of audio and then containing a second line that specifies how that can be modified to produce the left and right channels. Because music and vocals rarely differ much in the left and right channels, this manages to save a great deal of space — and the technique is even used by FM radio to broadcast music. If you want the utmost in quality, turn off Joint Stereo, but for most applications, Joint Stereo is a good idea.

As for filtering frequencies below 10 Hz, this is another space-saving feature. Very few people can hear — and even fewer speakers can reproduce — sounds below 10 Hz, so any space spent recording sounds that deep is wasted. However, some users report that, at very low bit-rates, in the range of 16kbps, turning off the 10 Hz filter can improve sound quality. However, not only is there no need to publish your podcast at such low quality, iTunes will not even allow you to try. Keep the 10 Hz filter turned on.

Creating a show template

Some of the busy work done in this chapter does not need to be repeated. Now that you have your fade ins and outs, jingles, post-production effects, and metadata, you should create a template that you can open instead of creating a new file each time you create a new episode. Click "File" and "Save As." Save your show with a name like "My Podcast Template."

Now, open the Finder and go to your home directory, "Music," and then "GarageBand." Right-click your template file, and choose "Get Info" from the context menu that appears. Check the box marked "Locked." From now on, when you open this file in GarageBand, all your post-production effects will already be setup for you, and all you need to do is save to a new file, hit the record button, and go.

Audacity

Shortcuts

Ctrl-Z	Undo Last Action
Ctrl-K	Delete
Ctrl-Alt-K	Split Delete
Ctrl-L	Silence Audio
Ctrl-X	Cut Audio
Ctrl-V	Paste Audio
Spacebar	Play Audio from cursor.

Audacity supports a more limited and focused set of features compared to GarageBand. There is no music synthesizer for creating your own jingles or a library of pre-existing, royalty-free jingles from which to choose. Many of the same sound enhancements supported by GarageBand are also in Audacity, but without the selection of easy-to-understand presets. *You can find a complete list of Audacity effects and how they work in Appendix E.*

Reduce noise

Audacity does have some features that GarageBand lacks; one of the most powerful and useful for a podcaster is the "Truncate Silence" feature available under the Effects menu. Open your recording and select that now. You can attempt to reduce the amount of ambient noise in an Audacity recording by using the "Noise Removal" option under the Effects menu. This is a two-step process. Highlight a silent area of the recording that presumably contains only the ambient noise. You can do this by clicking and dragging over a relatively quiet portion of the waveform with your mouse. The quiet portions will be those with an almost flat line. Once you have it selected, open the "Noise Removal" option box, and click "Get Noise Profile." The noise profile is analyzed by Audacity so it can get an idea of what noise in your environment sounds like. This analysis process will close the "Noise Removal" box while it works. Open it again and click "OK." Audacity will go through your recording and attempt to reduce noisy areas to absolute silence. It will even attempt, unlike the gate effect, to remove the presence of noise even during useful sound, like the host's voice. These effects are not perfect, but they are a powerful way to decrease the noise floor of your environment.

Stripping silent periods

In GarageBand, you had to manually go through and find any periods of prolonged silence, or dead air, during which you left the room, took a drink, or did something else. Audacity's "Truncate Silence" feature (found under the "Effects" menu) automates this process for you. The Truncate Silence dialog includes four settings: the minimum and maximum silence duration, the silence compression, and the threshold for silence. The minimum and maximum silence duration specifies how short the smallest silence should be and how long the longest silence should be. Each of these values must be at least one; minimum or maximum silences of zero will corrupt the recording. The silence compression dictates how much Audacity reduces silences that are too long. The higher the value, the more long silences will be compressed. Finally, the threshold shows how loud a section of audio can be and still be considered a silence. Leave the default settings and click "OK" in the "Truncate Silence" dialog. Any prolonged silent periods in your audio will be quickly and automatically cut down to a more reasonable length. If you discover on a quick listen that the results are not as you like, you can undo it and restore your recording to its pristine state by pressing Ctrl-Z.

Remove a section

If you need to manually remove a section of audio, because of a meowing cat or a passing airplane, you can do so easily. Simply locate the location of the sound and drag over it with your left mouse button down in the waveform editor. It will be highlighted, and you have three options: delete, split delete, and silence audio. Delete removes the offensive sound and moves the rest of the waveform to fill the empty space, leaving no pause. Split delete, on the other hand, leaves the deleted space completely blank, splitting the recording into two different audio clips that can be separately manipulated. Lastly, silence audio deletes the sound, but leaves a pause in the original audio. Unlike delete, it leaves a blank space for a pause, and unlike split delete, it does not split the recording into two different strips.

Add a pre-existing jingle

Audacity does not have its own selection of built-in jingles, but if you have your own, either as an MP3 or MIDI file, you can import it into Audacity by selecting "File," "Import," and either "Audio Data" or "MIDI." This will create a new track at the bottom of the page containing your jingle. To have it fade out, select that track and highlight the opening music section. Next, click "Effect" and "Fade Out."

Now, you will need to move your original recording over so that the start of your voice overlaps the fading out of the music. Click your original recording track and drag with your mouse to highlight it. Press "Ctrl-X" to cut the audio and then click the area of the track where you want your voice to enter and press "Ctrl-V" to paste. You can undo and paste again if you get it wrong. You can press the spacebar at any time to hear what it sounds like.

You can repeat the same process to add your jingle at the end. Simply import the jingle to a new track, highlight and cut it, and place it at the end. This time, you would highlight the jingle and use the "Fade In" effect. Do not recycle your old jingle for this purpose. Unlike GarageBand, Audacity modifies the sound data every time an effect, such as a fade out, is applied. To turn the fade out to a fade in, you need to reload the data from the disk in a new track.

To keep this straight, you can click the track name, click name, and give your tracks clearer names, such as "Opening Jingle" and "Closing Jingle."

Adding metadata

Metadata, the information embedded within the audio file that describes the episode content, is easy to add in Audacity. Simply click "File" and "Open Metadata Editor." Here, you will be presented with options to give the artist's name, the track title, the album title, the track number, year, genre, and comments. You should set the genre to "Podcast" and use the "Comments" tag for a short description of your show, but feel free to set other fields to any fitting information. A recommended method is to set the artist's name to your own name, the track title to the name of the current episode, and the album title to the name of your podcast.

Once you have set all this information, click the "Save" button under the "Template" heading. This will allow you to save the default information about your show to a template that you can load each time you create a new episode without the need to re-type your name and the name of your podcast.

Export to disk

Once you have finished with post-production and have added metadata to your file, it is time to export it to disc. This makes all the changes permanent, so be sure you are really finished before you do it. Click "File" and "Export." You will be given a choice of around a dozen different formats. For now, choose MP3. Click "Options."

The choices given to you under Audacity are more complex than the choices in GarageBand, but they amount to the same thing. You can choose between Stereo, which stores two completely separate audio channels for the left and right speakers, and Joint Stereo, which saves space by storing only one channel and only the minimum information needed to figure out the other channel at playtime. You are given a wider range of bit-rates: from as low as 8 kbps to as high as 320 kbps, with a default of 112. If your podcast is almost entirely spoken voice, you can safely go as low as 64 kbps, while even for extremely detailed and subtle music, you should not need to exceed 256 kbps to get a faithful rendition. Remember: the higher the setting, the more disk space and bandwidth your podcast will use. If all else fails, export your podcast at more than one setting, and use the one you think sounds best.

Finally, you can choose to go with a variable bit-rate, which will alter the quality as needed throughout the recording, with complex portions taking more space and simpler portions taking less. This saves some space while ensuring the quality is there when you need it, but a few older portable media players have limited support for variable bit-rate MP3 files.

Creating a show template

Now that you have made your first episode, you should create a template that will prevent much of the busy work in subsequent episodes. Be sure you save your work and select your main recording track and click "Edit," and "Silence Audio." This will remove your recording and leave only the jingles in place. Now click "File" and "Save Project As" and save a file with the name "My Podcast Template." From now on, you can simply open this file and record rather than starting from zero each time you do a show.

Chapter 7

How the Internet Works

This might be the best place to take some time and discuss how the technologies of the Internet are critical to your podcast work on a software level. Besides a few trivial aspects, there is no particular need for a podcaster to understand the Internet at the hardware level. Do not worry, this is not going to turn into a textbook on computer systems and architecture, but a podcaster that does not have at least a basic grasp of DNS or the different types of Web host services will make mistakes eventually — or pay a service exorbitant and unnecessary fees to do it for them. For a podcaster's purposes, the Internet can be divided into the following technologies:

- Web and file servers and clients
- RSS feeds
- DNS service
- Web and file servers

One potential source of confusion that should be cleared up immediately is what a podcast server really does. There is really no difference between a Web server and a podcast server. A podcast server is simply a website that has audio and/or video files along with a special file called the RSS feed. Therefore, when this chapter talks about Web servers, this applies to your podcast. You can even think of your podcast's RSS feed as just another type of website, designed to be read by computers instead of people.

A Web server actually can refer to two different things: a computer that holds a website and the application running on that computer that sends the website to people who ask for it. There is nothing particularly special about a server computer. *Chapter 9 discusses how to turn a home computer into a Web server*. Few podcasters choose that route, however, and instead contract services from a company with their own server farm — a facility of anywhere from dozens to thousands of computers that are leased out. A single computer in one of these farms can be responsible for serving anywhere from one to thousands of websites or podcasts. As you can probably imagine, the more podcasts that have to share a single server, the slower the performance is, with free services like Tripod having the slowest response, as a single computer must juggle thousands of websites, podcasts, and other Internet services at once. The old chestnut that you get what you pay for applies here, and paid services get gradually better as the price tag increases. Before we delve too deeply into your hosting options, however, you must learn what the host actually does.

Clients and Servers

Both of these terms are filled with potential for confusion because they can each refer to two different things. The word server can refer either to a computer program that responds to requests from

elsewhere on the Internet or the physical computer that holds that program. Likewise, the word client can refer either to the computer requesting information from the server or the program making the request on that computer. Most of the time, context will make clear which meaning of the word is being used. The most important thing to remember about the two words is this: The server is always the device (or program) that is answering a request or sending information, and the client is always the computer (or program) that is making the request and receiving information.

What a Server Does

The job of the server is actually extraordinarily simple at its most basic level. The server computer has a series of numbered ports on which it can listen for signals from the Internet. On the computer is a program, also called a server, which watches its assigned port and responds to any messages it receives. At the other end, a program on the end-user's computer, called a client, sends requests for the information it wants. Web browsers like Internet Explorer and podcatchers like iTunes are both examples of clients. Server software is less familiar to non-experts, but you might have heard of the Apache Web server used to host most websites and podcasts on the Internet. A typical transaction between a podcatcher and a podcast server will look like this. The client, iTunes, for example, will send a line of text over the Internet to the server. Web servers nearly all listen for signals on port number 80, so that is the port iTunes will use. At first, iTunes wants to know if there are any new episodes of the podcast, so it asks for a copy of the RSS feed, or the table of contents of the podcast. The request looks like this:

```
"GET WWW.MYPODCAST.COM/FEED.RSS"
```

The server receives the request and looks on its hard drive for a file named 'FEED.RSS,' and sends it back to iTunes. ITunes looks over the file and discovers that there are episodes in the table of contents that it does not possess, so, it checks the table of contents in FEED.RSS to discover the URL for that episode, and sends a new request, which looks like this:

```
"GET WWW.MYPODCAST.COM/01.MP3"
```

The server receives the new request and checks its hard drive again, this time looking for a file named "01.MP3," and sends the contents of the file back over the Internet to iTunes, which stores the file on its own hard drive until the user wants to listen to it.

Notice how this inverts the usual pattern for the distribution of media in other technologies. A television or radio station must constantly send information out over an antenna or a cable to emit its media signal. The televisions in our homes and radios in our cars are entirely passive: They always receive.

In podcasting (and all Web browsing, actually), the client, or the listener's computer, always asks for the specific information it would like to receive, and the server answers the request and immediately stops to await a new request. The server never simply sends the episode to be received by anyone with the equipment to listen. This should also relieve you a bit on the technical side of it. At an absolute minimum, all you need in a host is a reliable service to hold the RSS file and the episodes themselves, and most hosting services out there, from the cheap to the expensive, can do this for you.

Choosing a Server

As a podcaster, you will have five different choices when it comes to choosing a server to host your podcast. They are:

- Podcast shared hosting
- General shared hosting
- Dedicated hosting
- Virtual hosting
- Self hosting

Podcast-specific shared hosting

Podcast-specific shared hosts can be a great choice for the beginning podcaster because these services provide a one-size-fits-all solution to many technical issues a podcaster will face to get the show off the ground, such as creating and updating the RSS feed and providing a website. Typically, all that is needed for the podcast-shared hosts is to upload each episode to the server. The rest is handled automatically. Many even automatically handle the submission of your podcast to a variety of podcast directories.

However, this convenience comes with some pretty significant disadvantages. Most give you little to no control over the branding of the website they associate with your podcast; it tends to be nothing but a list of recent episodes on a one-size-fits-all layout, often with advertising injected into the page to help pay the host's bills. Many of the cheapest ones also have some shockingly stringent quotas for bandwidth and disk space, two resources that even small podcasts might chew through with alarming speed.

When considering a shared host with special features for podcasts, keep the following things in mind:

- **Bandwidth.** A weekly ten-minute audio podcast consumes about 40 to 50 megabytes of bandwidth per month per listener. Even the smallest and least successful podcasts tend to bring in a hundred listeners, which adds up to around five gigabytes of bandwidth per month. If your podcast becomes even moderately successful, expect to need a service willing to provide at least ten to 20 gigabytes of bandwidth per month without tacking on extra fees. If you plan to distribute a video podcast, you will need about ten times more than that.

- **Speed.** Even if a service assures you sufficient bandwidth each month, can its computers handle the strain? It is a common tactic with budget-shared hosts to promise the world in terms of bandwidth and disk space and then purchase nowhere near enough network speed to serve everyone. Find a few other podcasts hosted by the service and download their episodes. If the download speed seems particularly slow, only a few dozen kilobytes per second, consider another service.

- **Licenses.** Do they force you to distribute your content under a specific license, like the Creative Commons license? If so, make sure this is what you want. The license you distribute your content under is what sets the legal rights and responsibilities of you and your listeners. Some licenses amount to a more or less complete renunciation of your rights under copyright laws. *The Creative Commons license is discussed in greater deatil in Chapter 12.*

- **Ownership.** Who owns your podcast? Some free or cheap services assume ownership of the podcasts they host. Ensure that you maintain ownership of your own work.

- **Censorship.** Pornographic podcasts are banned from most of the major podcast directories and few hosts want to touch them due to the legal issues that surround their distribution, but some hosts implement far stricter standards than this and might refuse to host highly controversial topics.

- **Branding.** How much control will you have over the website for your podcast? Will you able to arrange your own advertising or affiliation programs? Will it be possible to create Web forums and other social networking features for your listeners?

- **Subdomains.** By default, many of these hosts do not allow you to have your own domain name, like www.mypodcast.com, and instead force you to be content with a mere subdomain, like www.mypodcast.podbean.com, unless you pay a little more money.

Generic shared hosting

General shared hosting is similar to podcast-specific hosting; it has all the disadvantages without the extra features for podcasting. In practice, the services provided by podcast-specific hosts are easy enough to handle for yourself, but generic shared hosting has a few disadvantages of its own, including:

- **Bandwidth.** Most generic shared hosting plans assume their customers are going to use their service for ordinary text and picture-driven Web pages, so they are unlikely to provide enough bandwidth for a podcast.

- **Format limits.** To curb music and movie piracy, many shared hosts place strict limits on which types of files can be placed on their service, banning formats like MP3, AVI, and MPEG — exactly the formats you are most likely to need for your show.

Dedicated hosting

At the opposite end of the spectrum from shared hosting is dedicated hosting. If a Web service has the full resources of a single machine to itself, that machine is known as a dedicated host. Extremely popular services, those that depend on complex or demanding database-driven Web applications, simply cannot share a computer with other services. Dedicated hosting provides the greatest performance of all hosting options available and has another advantage: added control. Customers who purchase a dedicated host can make every decision about their server, from which operating system it runs to how the software is configured.

However, all that power comes with a disadvantage: cost. Typical dedicated hosts cost hundreds of dollars per month to keep online, which is simply beyond the means of even the most successful podcasts. The other significant disadvantage is complexity. Because dedicated hosting is beyond the price range of casual users and hobbyists, dedicated hosting services assume their clients will have an entire IT department to keep them running.

Virtual hosting

The middle ground between shared hosting and dedicated hosting in recent years is the virtual host. A virtual hosting service allows each website or podcast to run inside a special program, called a virtual machine, which pretends to be an entire computer. A single computer might run dozens of virtual machines at once, each with its own operating system, installed programs, and settings. Technically, this is a form of shared hosting, but the technology allows multiple services to share a computer while providing each with the illusion that it has the machine entirely to itself.

Publishers can do anything on the machine they would be able to do with a machine in their living room, including installing new programs or operating systems and changing system-wide settings. Many of these systems even take advantage of cloud-computing technology, which allows a podcast producer to pay to increase only the resources, such as processing power or bandwidth that they want, up to and even beyond the capacities of a dedicated host, without paying for the extra features they do not need. Some, like Google's App Engine service or Amazon Elastic Compute Cloud, provide you with the full resources of the company's computers and only charge you for what you use, unlike a dedicated host, in which a system has been set aside at all times, which you must pay for, even if it sits idle. They do keep one disadvantage of the dedicated host: They can be complicated to use, and some, like the Google Application Engine, require a great deal of technical savvy to use.

Self-hosting

There is one last option: self-hosting. A server computer is really just an ordinary computer that runs a program that listens for messages from the Internet and responds with information. The most common, and arguably most powerful, Web server software, Apache, is completely free, both for commercial and noncommercial use, and can be downloaded from the Apache Foundation's website at **www.apache.org**. With self-hosing, you have complete control. Want advertisements? Add them. Want a forum for your listeners? Build it. Want to only have three episodes up at a given time? Do it.

Also, after you have the computer and have paid your Internet Service Provider (ISP), with self-hosting, there are no other fees. Take up as much or as little space as you want. Use as much of your own bandwidth as it takes. You are getting a dedicated host for the price of your Internet connection.

But with these advantages come disadvantages as well, including:

- **Security.** A computer is normally configured to do its best to reject any information from the Internet that it does not remember asking for. In fact, if it receives information it did not want, the computer does its absolute best to act as if it does not exist, in the hopes that an attacking hacker or virus will give up rather than waste their time attacking a nonexistent computer. Turning the computer into a server leaves all that behind. Not only is the computer no longer hiding, but it is using the DNS system to advertise its own existence. You might as well paint a big red target on it. If you go the self-hosting route, your computer will be attacked by hackers, par-

ticularly if you have something to say in your podcast that others might not like. Expect to spend a fair amount of time becoming an expert in computer security.

- **Upstream bandwidth.** ISPs advertise their Internet speeds in terms of downstream bandwidth, the speed at which your computer can receive information from the Internet, and typically offer a dramatically reduced rate for upstream bandwidth, the rate at which data can be sent, or uploaded, to other computers. A three-megabits-per-second residential connection might only have 128-kilobits-per-second of upstream bandwidth, which is shockingly insufficient, especially if your podcast includes video or has more than a few dozen listeners.

- **ISP contracts.** Some ISPs simply do not allow their residential customers to operate servers. Before deciding to go the self-hosting route, check your contract to determine whether you are barred from operating a server from your home. If so, you might need to contact your ISP to upgrade to a (more expensive) business-oriented service plan.

- **Dynamic IP.** Even if your ISP does not bar you from self-hosting explicitly, they might use dynamic IP. The IP is the actual number that identifies your computer's location on the Internet. For a self-hosted service to be reliable, it is very important that it have an IP address that does not change (otherwise known as a static IP), but if your ISP uses dynamic IPs, it might shuffle up the addresses every now and then, which will break your Web service until you can fix the problem.

- **Reliability.** Internet and power outages are a nuisance; however, if you elect to self-host, they will affect your podcast. Any time the computer holding your podcast server cannot access the Internet (or is turned off), listeners will receive error messages that your podcast or its website no longer exist.
- **Complexity.** There is no technical support to go to for help when you elect to do it yourself. You could, however, always hire professionals to set up your server and perform maintenance as needed. Elance (**www.elance.com**), Freelancer (**www.freelancer.com**), and oDesk (**www.odesk.com**) provide a valuable resource for finding these professionals.

There is No Such Thing as a Free Lunch

People unfamiliar with open-source software might be a bit suspicious of quality software offered free of charge. Why is Apache free? If it is so great, why it is it free?

Many software companies that produce software for business, including those that produce both open-source and closed-source software, derive a large portion of their income from elaborate support contracts rather than the fees they get from sales. If you have ever waited on hold for tech support, only to be taken through a litany of questions like "Is your computer plugged in?" once you finally get on the phone with a person, you probably understand why a company might be willing to pay fees to jump straight to the front of the line and skip the nonsense. Indeed, many sponsors of the Apache Foundation, such as Spring Source, make their money by selling technical support and training for the software.

If you are of an idealistic disposition, much of open source is driven by a philosophy that suggests that because producing extra copies of software costs nothing, the software should be free. Whether you find that philosophy alluring or not, many talented programmers do, and they produce a great deal of software every year.

On the other hand, if you are of a cynical disposition, you might look through the list of companies that sponsor the Apache Foundation and notice a conspicuous absence: Microsoft. Some analysts argue that the success of open-source software is driven partially by companies that stand to lose big if Microsoft controls both server and browser technology. So, they give away software like Apache and the Firefox browser as a way to ensure their own Internet-based businesses never become too dependent on the whims of their competitor, Microsoft.

The real reasons why the old adage about the free lunch and getting what you pay for does not apply to open-source software like Apache are probably a mix of all of the above, but the important thing to take away is that there really is quality, free software out there that can help with your podcast, especially if you choose the self-hosting option.

DNS

The domain name system (DNS) network is the unsung hero of the Internet. Without it, the Internet would be almost unusable for all but computer scientists and engineers. The service takes a URL address like **www.google.com** and converts it to something computers can actually use to find one other: the IP address. The IP address for Google looks like this: 74.125.95.104. The technical side is not really important, but one thing is critical: If you want your own domain name, like **www.mypodcast.com**, then you are going to need to purchase that domain name and register it in the domain name system with your IP. Most Web hosting services will take care of this for you (some even offer discount rates on domain names), but if you adopt the self-hosting route, you will be on your own in this regard.

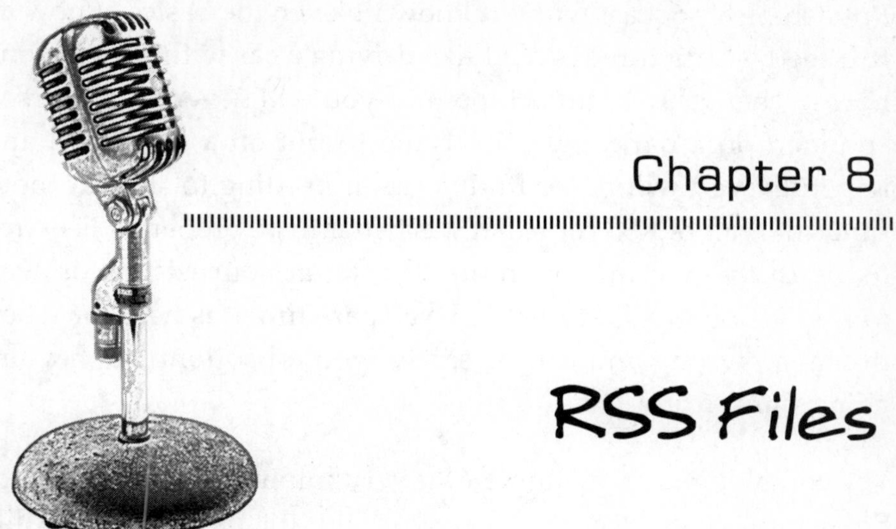

Chapter 8

RSS Files

The Really Simple Syndication (RSS) feed is one of the key technologies to podcast distribution. It is a simple file, written in the XML computer language. The best metaphor for an RSS file is a table of contents, or even a card catalog in a library, which is designed to be read by a computer. It contains a list of podcast episodes with details on what the episodes are and how a computer program can find them.

We went over RSS feeds briefly in the Introduction, and you will almost certainly want to choose a tool that will handle the construction and maintenance of the RSS feed for you. Even computer experts who know XML and RSS syntax like the back of their hands use tools like these to handle RSS feeds. However, no self-respecting podcaster should be without a basic knowledge of how the feed itself works. This is the heart of your podcast, and if something goes wrong, it is most likely to go wrong here.

Publishing a podcast without knowing even the basics of how an RSS feed is structured is a bit like driving a car without knowing how to change a flat tire. Hopefully, you will never find yourself stranded on a dark highway trying to put on a spare tire, and hopefully you will never find yourself needing to stare at thousands of lines of RSS code, but it is better to be prepared. Feel free to digest the information in this chapter at your leisure, or even to skip it on your first read. Like a spare tire, it is here for when things go wrong and can be safely ignored so long as they are going right.

The following is an example of a very minimalist podcast feed. Before you go on, see if you can work out the purpose of the different tags, the RSS commands inside the arrow brackets '< >', in the feed for yourself.

A Sample RSS Feed

```
 <?xml version="1.0" encoding="UTF-8"?>
 <rss version="2.0" xmlns:ds="http://www.
mypodcast.com/index.html</link>
        <description> Now at any time, day
or night, you can stay up late with Steven
Winters as he talks to guests about poli-
tics, celebrities, and the popular cu@ </de-
scription>
        <language>en-us</language>
        <copyright>Steve Winters. All
Rights Reserved</copyright>
        <item>
```

```
            <title>Iron Man Versus Freddy
Krueger</title>
            <link>http://www.mypod-
cast.com/Episode-103IronManVsFreddy.MP3"
length="10298132" type="audio/mpeg"/>
        </item>
    </channel>
</rss>
```

It is not exactly English, but it is probably easier to understand than you anticipated. Besides a few tags that serve technical purposes like xmlns and encoding, most of them have easy to understand names like title, pubDate, and description. First, a channel (or podcast) is given a title, description, and a link to a Web page for the podcast. Then, individual items (or episodes) are described, which also have a title and a description. They also have a Web link, but instead of directing to a Web page, these tell the listener's computer where it can find the episode file – an MP3 in this case. This example shows only one episode, but an RSS feed for a mature podcast can contain hundreds of <item> tags, each representing a different episode. *Later, this chapter will go into more detail about which commands (or tags) are required and which are supported in the RSS file for your podcast.* Any time you publish a new broadcast for your podcast, you or your podcast host will do two things. First, they will upload an audio or a video file of your podcast to an Internet server where listeners can access it. Second, they will update the RSS feed with information about the new podcast by adding a new <item> tag with all its information. At minimum, it will include information about where the listener's computer should look to get the new episode, its title, and the date and time that the episode was uploaded.

Delving a Little Deeper

Look at the sample podcast RSS feed in the previous section again, and pay special attention to the indentation, or the amount of white space that is located to the left of each line of the code. This indentation is not strictly necessary; the computer will understand the code even if it looks like this:

```
<?xml version="1.0" encoding="UTF-8"?> <rss
version="2.0" xmlns:ds="http://www.mypod-
cast.com/"> <channel> <title>Up Late With
Steve Winters</title> <link>http://www.my-
podcast.com/index.html</link> <description>
Now at any time, day or night, you can stay
up late with Steven Winters as he talks to
guests about politics, celebrities, and the
popular cu@ </description> <language>en-
us</language> <copyright>Steve Winters.
All Rights Reserved</copyright> <item>
<title>Iron Man Versus Freddy Krueger</
title> <link> http://www.mypodcast.com/Epi-
sode-103IronManVsFreddy.MP3</link> <descrip-
tion> In this episode, Steve discusses the
latest movies with Annah Carlin, film critic
for the Springfield Daily Post. (Running
Time 10:54) </description> <pubDate>Tue,
17 May 2010 17:11:49 GMT</pubDate> <enclo-
sure url="http://www.mypodcast.com/Episode-
103IronManVsFreddy.MP3" length="10298132"
type="audio/mpeg"/> </item> </channel> </
rss>
```

The purpose of the indentation is to reveal a feature of the RSS feed commands to a human reader. They are nested. For example, one of the first tags that occurs in an RSS feed will always be the <rss> tag, and one of the last tags, if not the very last tag, in the feed will be the </rss> tag. The first is known as an opening tag, and the latter is known as a closing tag. You can always recognize the closing tag because it will have a forward slash in it somewhere. Together, the opening and closing <rss> tags let the computer know where the RSS feed begins and ends. To make it easier for a human reader looking at the feed (to find out why his or her podcast has suddenly broken after a recent update, for example), everything within these two tags is indented a few spaces to the right.

Immediately within the <rss> tags are the <channel> tags. Again, you should notice that a <channel> tag is located near the top of the RSS file, which is used to open the channel, and a </channel> tag is located near the bottom to close the channel. Within the RSS file, each podcast is its own channel. In practice, this is a little redundant. A single RSS feed should never have more than one channel. Think about it this way: The <rss> tag lets the computer know that the feed is an RSS feed, and the <channel> tag lets the computer know that the information within is actually about the podcast.

At an absolute minimum, the channel tag must contain three more tags. Those are the <title>, <link>, and <description> tags. The <title> tag and its closer </title> hold the title of the entire podcast. The <description> tag and its closer </description> hold a short description of the podcast, and the <link> tag and its closer </link> hold a Web link to the podcast's homepage on the World Wide Web. If you were to upload a minimal RSS file containing this information, <rss>, <channel>, <title>, <description>, and <link>, podcatcher software like iTunes would be able to recognize it. The following RSS feed for a podcast contains the minimum needed for a valid podcast feed:

```
<?xml version="1.0" encoding="UTF-8"?>
<rss version="2.0"">
    <channel>
        <title>An Empty Podcast</title>
         <link>http://www.mypodcast.com/in-
dex.html</link>
        <description> A podcatcher like
iTunes can read this podcast feed file. How-
ever, since there are no item tags, it sees
it as a podcast without any episodes! </de-
scription>
    </channel>
</rss>
```

However, the podcast referenced by this feed would appear empty to iTunes. To assign episodes, the <item> tag must be used — along with its closer. For every episode of the podcast, a new <item> tag will be opened and closed (</item>). A long-running podcast may have hundreds of <item> open tags and </item> close tags in it. Like the <channel> tag, each <item> tag gets its own <title>, <description>, and <link> tags, but it also has a few others. The most important of these are the <enclosure> and the <guid> tags.

<enclosure> tag

The first is a special tag used by podcasting software to identify the location of the podcast episode itself and looks like the following:

```
<enclosure
   url="http://www.mypodcast.com/Epi-
 sode-103IronManVsFreddy.MP3"
 length="10298132"
   type="audio/mpeg"/>
```

Do not be thrown off by the alternative style this example uses. Instead of an </enclosure> closing tag, it is just placing the closing forward slash at the very end. This is perfectly acceptable. However, the enclosure tag does have a few more parts than the other tags dealt with in this chapter: a URL, a length, and a type. All three of these are necessary.

The URL is simple enough; it gives the Web address where the podcatcher software can find the episode to download. The length is the expected size of the episode in bytes. Finally, the type is the file type of the episode. If you have a podcast distributed using MP3 audio files, chances are your feed will look similar to "audio/mpeg." The codes used to describe these are called MIME types, and you must choose a valid MIME type for your podcast to work. The following chart gives you some examples of common MIME types used in podcasts:

MIME Type	File Types
audio/mpeg	.MP3
audio/x-m4a	.M4A
video/mp4	.MP4
video/x-m4v	.M4V
video/quicktime	.MOV

<guid> tag

The <guid> tag, or the Global Unique Identifier, is intended to be something like your tag's social security number. The goal is that this tag should contain a string of characters that is unique to each episode in your podcast. Leaving the <guid> tag out will result in only one episode from your podcast appearing in some podcatchers. Mistakes within the <guid> tag could also cause other episodes to mysteriously disappear. The easiest way to deal with this mischievous tag is simple: Just give it the same definition as the <link> tag. Because each episode will presumably have a unique link to download it, you can rest assured the <guid> tag will always be unique.

The XML declaration tag

You might have noticed that all the example feeds start with a tag that looks something like this: <?xml version="1.0" encoding="UTF-8"?>. This line is necessary to let the podcatcher know that the feed is written in the XML language, which version of XML is used, and which method the XML file is using to convert, or encode, letters into computer data. Nearly all podcasts will use an XML declaration tag that looks almost exactly the one given here.

Other Important Tags in a Podcast Feed

So far, all of the essential tags for a functioning podcast have been covered. In order to work without errors, a podcast must have a properly nested set of <rss>, <channel>, <description>, <link>, and <title> tags. Each episode of the podcast, in turn, must also have its own <item>, <description>, <title>, <link>, and <enclosure> tags. These are the absolute minimum for a podcast to function, but there are a few more tags you will want to include in your podcast. All of these tags are optional, but they add extra bells and whistles to the podcast feed that you will very likely not want to do without.

<pubDate> tag

The <pubDate> tag goes inside the <tag> and holds the date and time that the most recent episode was published. It is mostly self-explanatory except for one caveat; because the date must be something a computer can read and understand, it follows a very strict format called RFC 822. If you feel technically inclined, you can go to http://asg.web.cmu.edu/rfc/rfc822.html to read the description of the format. Here is what the tag itself looks like: <pubDate>Mon, 14 Jan 2010 12:45:03 -0800</pubDate>.

<language> tag

The <language> tag is not required, but it is a nice thing to add to your podcast feed. It tells podcast listeners — and more importantly, podcast directories — which language the podcast content will be in. Like the <pubDate> tag, the <language> tag has a strict format so computers can read it, and each language used on Earth, in addition to most major dialects within languages, has its own code. The code for American English, for example, is "en-us." If you are interested in a complete list of the codes, either because you want to host a foreign language podcast or because you are simply curious, you can read them at Harvard Law's website at http://cyber.law.harvard.edu/rss/languages.

html. For example, the following is the RSS tag to identify a podcast as using American English:

```
<language>en-us</language>
```

<copyright> tag

The <copyright> tag gives you a nifty place to declare the copyright licensing scheme that you have decided to use for your podcast. *Chapter 10 will go into some popular licenses for podcast producers, along with their advantages and disadvantages.* If there is any doubt, the following works well, with the year adjusted to the date of publication: <copyright>Copyright 2010 All Rights Reserved</copyright>. However, you are not required to include this tag. If you do not elect to use a broader license, such as the Creative Commons, then it is solely for informational purposes. U.S. copyright law provides your podcast the broadcast possible protection by default.

<image> tag

The <image> tag is a tag you definitely do not want to leave out of your podcast's RSS feed. This will allow your podcast to have an image, similar to album art, attached to it in supporting podcatchers and MP3 players. The following is an example of how the image tag usually looks:

```
<image> <width>144</width> <height>144</
height> <link> www.mypodcast.com</link>
<title>My Podcast</title> <url> www.mypod-
cast.com/images/podcast.jpg</url> </image>
```

As you might suspect, the <link> and <title> tags provide a link to your podcast's home page on the World Wide Web and the

title of the show, respectively. On the other hand, the <width> and <height> tags provide the width and height, in pixels, of the image. This is known as the image's resolution. You might need to duplicate this content a little bit later, however, as iTunes does not support the <image> tag. Instead, you will need to use the <itunes:image> tag described in the next section of this chapter.

iTunes-specific Tags

Apple's iTunes is currently the premier location for podcasting, and unfortunately, that means they get to write a few of their own rules when it comes to the podcasting game. To have a podcast that will function correctly within the iTunes podcast directory, you will want to include the following tags in your RSS feed. A few of them duplicate the functionality of the tags above.

<itunes:subtitle> tag

The <itunes:subtitle> tag is like a mini-description of your podcast. It needs to be only a sentence or two in length at the most, and it will be used as the default description of every episode in your podcast, just in case you release one that does not have its own description. Here is what it looks like: <itunes:subtitle>A great show about clouds!</itunes:subtitle>.

The <itunes:summary> tag describes two things: inside the <channel> tag, it holds the description of your podcast itself, and inside each <item> tag, it will hold the description for the individual episodes. In either case, you get a total of 4,000 characters to write a description here. The summary tag should look like this: <itunes:summary>. The cloud show is a weekly podcast about all the great ways clouds affect our lives and our culture, hosted by Charles McLoward.</itunes:summary>.

The <itunes:owner> tag allows you to give credit to the owner of the podcast, particularly if this person differs from the author. It is a straightforward tag to use and looks like this: <itunes:owner>Kevin Walker</itunes:owner>. It should be placed inside the <channel> tag section of the podcast's RSS feed.

As you might suppose, the author allows you to specify the podcast's author. For most producers, this will read the same as the <itunes:owner> tag, but if you need to give separate credit to each individual, the option is available.

This tag is used to attach album art to a podcast's episode. The standard RSS image tag limits the resolution to a maximum of 144x400 pixels, a fairly bizarre size and not one that works well with the design of iTunes software. To fix this, Apple has created the <itunes:image> tag, with a maximum size of 300x300 pixels. To be safe, your podcast should include both the <image> and <itunes:image> tags. The syntax for the tag is much simpler than the syntax for the standard image tag as well. It simply reads:

```
<itunes:image>http://www.mypodcast.com/im-
agefile.jpg</itunes:image>
```

Apple is pretty conservative about what it will allow on iTunes and what it expects to be flagged as explicit. Any content that could conceivably land Apple in legal trouble is not allowed. That means no pornography or erotica, nothing that might be considered hate speech, and no illegal solicitations, such as advertisements for a brothel. Apple does not consider them explicit; they are banned immediately.

Rather, the <itunes:explicit> tag should be used for podcasts that use foul language or include content that, while not pornographic, is still somewhat adult in nature. Do not think of the explicit tag as analogous to an NC-17 or R-rating for a movie. Think of it as closer to a PG-13 or even a PG rating. A good rule of thumb: If you say anything that would have bothered your mother when you were 10, you should probably add an explicit tag. This is what the explicit tag looks like when turned on:

```
<itunes:explicit>yes</itunes:explicit>
```

And when turned off:

```
<itunes:explicit>no</itunes:explicit>
```

<itunes:keywords> tag

The <itunes:keywords> tag is one of the most important tags in the iTunes set. This tag allows you to select up to a dozen words that the iTunes search engine can use to direct users to your podcast. For example, if you have a podcast about New England bird watching, you might want to include the following <itunes:keywords> tag in your podcast's RSS feed to drive more traffic to your site: <itunes:keywords>New England birdwatching birds Maine Vermont birdwatcher Jersey York Connecticut</itunes:keywords>.

How iTunes will use the tags

ITunes will use the words in the summary, title, subtitle, and keywords tags to deliver users to the podcasts they search for, which means you should put some thought into what you put in these tags. *SEO practices will be covered in Chapter 11, and you should apply them here.*

But there is one pretty big caveat: Just like Google, Apple does not care for people playing black hat SEO games with its iTunes search engine. If they catch you stuffing your descriptions with unintelligible gibberish made up of popular keywords or using descriptions that have nothing to do with your podcast (but contain popular search terms anyway), they will permanently ban your podcast from the iTunes directory.

RSS Feed Building Software

Most hosting solutions, from Podbean to Wordpress, will generate the RSS feed automatically when you upload to their service without any effort from you. However, services that support this feature can be a little expensive, and there is absolutely nothing about an RSS feed that requires an expensive host to support it. After all, to a Web host, an RSS feed is nothing more than a specially formated text-file. If you would prefer to go with a cheaper hosting solution and just generate the RSS file yourself, you can use RSS feed building software. There are a number of solutions out there, but one good program is Podcast Generator (http://podcastgen.sourceforge.net), a free and open-source program. Just give it the information on your episodes, and it saves an RSS file ready to be uploaded to your chosen host.

Feed verification

Whether your write your feed by hand, use feed building software, or depend on your Web host to perform the service for you, feed verification should be a regular step you perform each time you update your podcast with a new episode. The easiest way to do this is to use the free online service FEED Validator (http://feedvalidator.org). Go to the website, enter the URL for your podcast's

RSS feed into the box, and press the "Validate" button. If everything checks out, you will get a congratulations and the assurance of knowing that your podcast is functioning with any standards-compliant podcatching software. If there is an error, it will tell you the problems, and you will either need to fix them yourself or send a polite letter to your Web host about the problem.

A Few Last Words

If something goes wrong with your podcast, the RSS feed is probably going to be the source of the trouble, and there are a few things in particular that you will need to watch out for when building your feed.

The beginning of the chapter talked a little about the encoding tag, which is the tag at the very top of the RSS file that tells the computer which method to use to convert the electronic information, or the sequence of cryptic 0s and 1s received from the Internet, into letters, numbers, and punctuation symbols. Chances are that unless you are a programmer, you have not had to worry about encoding methods. When most people wish to enter some text on theirs computers, they just type everything in Microsoft Word and let the computer worry about how it is stored and transmitted. Most of the time, that is OK, but when working with RSS feeds, Microsoft Word can throw things for a loop, because it uses all sorts of characters that a podcatcher like iTunes is not going to know how to understand. For example, in order to improve the visual quality of documents, Microsoft Word uses different characters for opening and closing quotes. It is a great feature, but those characters are not a part of the text encoding formats that most podcatchers (including iTunes) understand. Should you copy a bit of text from Microsoft Word containing those quotes into an RSS file or an automated RSS generator, these characters will appear as gibberish to your listeners, and they can even break the podcast's RSS feed itself. If you choose to work with RSS files yourself, it is imperative you stick to using Notepad or a programming text editor like Notepad++ (for Windows) or TextWrangler (for Mac OS X). Word processing programs like Microsoft Word, Open Office, or Apple Pages are great programs for writing content intended to be read by humans, but they are not good choices for writing content that must be understood by other computer programs.

Although it is technically possible to have thousands upon thousands of episodes in your podcast, in practice, podcatchers start to break down if a podcast's RSS file exceeds 256 kilobytes in size. The amount of space that each episode takes up in the RSS feed could range anywhere from a few hundred to a thousand bytes. That means, after your podcast has more than a hundred or so episodes, you will approach a point where more updates will break the podcast. If you only want a recent selection of episodes online at a given time, this should not be a problem for your show, but if you want the entire library to be available to your listeners, you might need an alternative method of distribution for older episodes.

The last position problem is duplicate <guid> tags. You will remember from earlier in the chapter that the <guid> tag should contain some text that uniquely identifies every episode. If you keep your <guid> tags equal to the link where a user can download your podcast, then you should never have to deal with the duplicate <guid> error, but it is worth repeating. If two episodes of your podcast share the same <guid> tag, the result will be a broken podcast that will cease to work with your listener's computers.

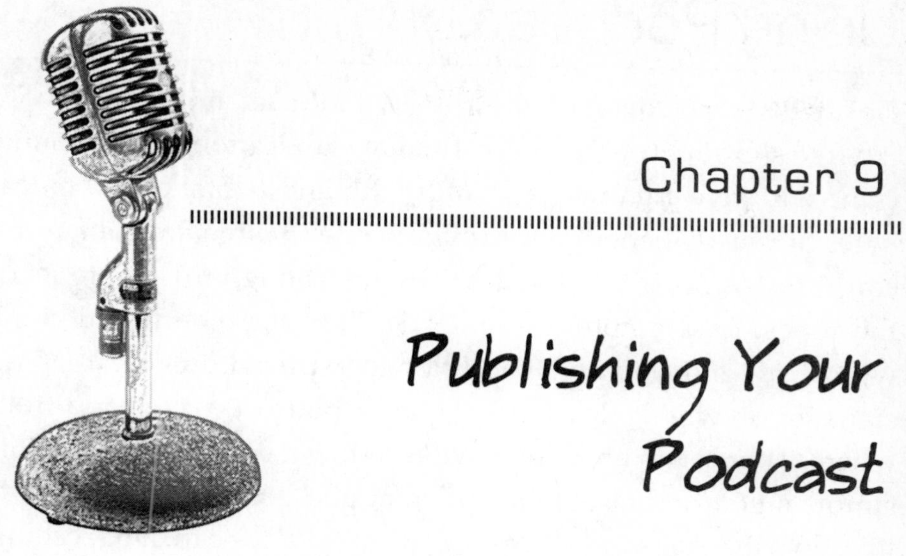

Chapter 9

Publishing Your Podcast

You have recorded your first show, put it through the paces of post-production, and gotten the skinny on how podcasting works from a technical standpoint. Now, it is time to put your show out into the world of eager listeners. In Chapter 7, we talked about five or six different hosting methods you can use for your podcast. In this chapter, you will go through the paces of both the easiest hosting method and the most difficult. You will set up a free account on Podbean.com, a dedicated podcast hosting service with both free and paid service plans, and you will setup your own personal computer as a self-host for your podcast using the Bitnami distribution of WordPress and the PodPress plugin. Both options will be initially free, though you will be up to you to decide which you prefer and make it the real hosting solution for your show. It is recommended that you follow both sets of instructions to get a feel for each path before making a final choice for your hosting decisions.

Using Podbean.com

Go to Podbean.com website (**http://podbean.com**) and choose the free sign-up option. At the time of publication, free accounts came with five gigabytes of bandwidth and a total of 100 megabytes of space – enough for roughly one to three hours of audio content. It is not a lot of space, but it is enough for you to learn the ropes. Paid accounts start at $2.49 a per month and come with vastly more space, in addition to extra features for keeping statistics on who is downloading your podcast, when, and from where. There is no need to go with Podbean.com forever, but it is simply a good representative of what podcast-specific hosting is like, and the skills you learn on your free Podbean.com account will carry over to any new hosting service you choose.

To signup, you are going to be asked for a username, and this will be used for the URL for your podcast's Web page by default, so choose something fitting for your podcast. It will need to be a valid Web address however, so do not use spaces or special characters like & or # and it should not exceed more than a dozen letters or numbers. The site asks for a valid e-mail, your name, address, date of birth, and gender. You can only have one free account per e-mail address, however, so keep that in mind.

Set a theme

Once you receive your confirmation email and activate your account with your new password, you will be taken to the dashboard for your service, from which you can add and remove episodes and edit the settings for your podcast and its website. There will not be much in it, but you can see what your Web page looks like by default by going to your new URL, which will follow this format: http://USERNAME.podbean.com. You should insert the username you created into the Web address. Before doing anything else, click the "Layout" tab. Here, you can browse different website layouts and choose the one that most appeals to you. You should choose the one that best fits the tone of your site.

Next, choose the "Sidebar Widgets" tab, and select the items you would like to appear at the side of your Web page. Available widgets include a widget for receiving PayPal donations, a list of links, and a search box. Select any of these you would like to use. If the widget has a small menubox next to it, you can click that to set its options. For example, for "PayPal Donate," you need to set the default donation amount and the e-mail address associated with your PayPal account.

Setting your show details

Click "Settings" from the menu bar, and you will be given a wealth of options for the description of your show, including the chance to upload an episode logo, set your podcasts privacy (whether it is visible to everyone or only a select group of friends), and add your show name and some keywords to make your podcast easier to find in the search engines. Be sure to fill in all the options on this page. The keywords are especially important, as they are how others will find your show.

Uploading an episode

Click the "Publish" tab, and you will be taken to the post upload screen. Here, you will set a description, a title, the episode, and the tags for your show. Let's do tags first.

Tags are keywords: short phrases and words that describe your show to make it easier for people to find it using search engines. *See Chapter 11 on SEO for more advice on how to choose good keywords*. For now, pick the major words in your episode title and description, separated by commas. For example, a show on cross-country cycling might use the keywords "cross-country cycling," "bicycling," and "off-road bikes."

Once you have filled in your tags, title, and show description, click the "Choose File" button to upload the MP3 file from your hard drive that contains your podcast. The upload might take anywhere from a few seconds to a few minutes, depending on the speed of your Internet connection and the size of your show. Once it is finished, click the "Show" button next to "Post specific settings for iTunes" to ensure that the iTunes specific RSS tags are as expected.

Click "Publish," and your show is online. Go to your unique URL to see what it looks like to Web browsers.

Get on iTunes

One of the advantages of Podbean.com and other podcast-specific hosts is how easy they make it to get onto the iTunes network. Click the "Feed/iTunes" tab and fill in all the information you are asked for. Only one option should be mysterious: the request for the FeedID for your show. The simplest way to get this information is to open iTunes and choose "Submit a Podcast" from the iTunes Store's podcast section. You will only be asked for one piece of information: the RSS feed URL given on the Podbean.com "Feed/iTunes" page. After you enter that information, iTunes will check to ensure that the podcast really exists

and contains at least one episode, and you will be asked to select categories for your podcast. It will take a few hours to a few days for your podcast to appear in the iTunes store after this, as it must be approved by an Apple employee. When you are accepted, you will receive a FeedID that you can enter into the settings page on Podbean.com.

Check statistics

Click the "Statistics" tab to get some info on how many people are tuning in for your podcast. You will be surprised at how quickly your listener base will grow, especially after it is accepted to the iTunes directory. Right now, however, your statistics will likely be at zero. However, it can be an exhilarating experience to check back on your show every few weeks and see how its popularity has grown.

You now have a podcast hosted on the free section of the dedicated podcast host Podbean.com. Though the interface will change from host to host, the essential features and steps will stay the same no matter which podcasting host you use. Feel free to shop around and find a service that meets your needs at the best price.

Self Hosting: Using WordPress & Blubrry Powerpress

At the other end of the spectrum from dedicated podcast hosting services like Podbean.com is self-hosting. With self-hosting, you do everything yourself on your own home computer. The advantage is that you do not need to pay hosting fees, but there are a number of technical disadvantages, including that your podcast and its Web page will go down immediately when ever your computer is shutdown or loses its Internet connection.

This tutorial will use the free Content Management System (CMS) WordPress and the free Blubrry PowerPress plugin to grant WordPress support for podcasting. You can download an easy installation file for WordPress from the BitNami service at **http://bitnami.org/stack/wordpress**. Alternatively, you can go to the WordPress home page at **www.wordpress.org** (not to be confused with WordPress.com, a blogging service that uses the WordPress program). Downloads are prepared for Windows, Linux, and both x86 and PPC versions of the Mac operating system. Each will take approximately 50 megabytes of space on your hard drive. Use all the default options for the installer until you reach the admin account page. On this page, you will need to choose a username and password for your administrator account. Because this will go live on the Internet and will give complete control over the podcast to anyone who can enter it, you should put some thought into a strong password. Choose one that contains both uppercase and lowercase letters as well as numbers. The further you can get from a real word found in a dictionary the stronger your password will be.

After this, you will be asked for the name of your podcast and the hostname for your show. Leave it with the default value for now. The installation will take a few minutes to run. Once it finishes, your browser will open the home page for your site. Click "Log In" and provide your username and password. You will be taken directly to the site administration panel. It can look a bit overwhelming at first, but do not worry. We will go through it step by step.

Set a theme

Click the "Appearance" button on the left side of the administration panel to go to the themes area. You will only have one theme on your system at first, but the process of installing more themes is heavily automated. Click the "Install Themes" tab. You will be given a search box. If you like, you can enter a color or other word that describes what you would like your podcast's Web page to look like, but the easiest way is just to choose the "Featured" option and select a theme from the list. Once you find one you like, just click "Install." An automated script will run, and you will be presented with the chance to preview the theme applied to your site or activate it immediately. Choose "Activate." If you decide you do not like the theme after all, you can change it at anytime.

Now click "Widgets." Just like with Podbean.com, this gives you a choice of dozens of widgets you can place in the side menu of your site. One very important widget is the "RSS" widget. This provides an easy way for listeners to subscribe to your RSS feed if they do not use the iTunes directory to manage their podcasts.

Enable podcasting

Out of the box, WordPress comes with most of the features needed for a podcast. Most importantly, all posts made to WordPress are automatically added to a valid RSS feed, eliminating the need for you to work with RSS code yourself in all but the most dramatic of circumstances. However, there is one major thing lacking: support for podcast-specific RSS tags. This is a dramatic shortcoming, as you need the iTunes specific tags to use the iTunes podcast directory — the location where listeners are most likely to find your show. This functionality is provided by a number of free add-ons to Word Press, but here we will use Blubrry PowerPress. Blubrry PowerPress is a free plugin maintained by the podcast host and advertising network Blubrry; however, you do not need to be a member of Blubrry to use their plugin. You can use other plugins as well, and another popular choice is PodPress. You can read more about it at **www.blubrry.com/powerpress**. Ignore the download link, however. There is an easier way to install Power-Press than the manual download.

In the WordPress administration panel, click "Plugins" and "Add New." Type "podcast" and click "Install Now" under the "Blubrry PowerPress Podcasting Plugin" result. An automated process will run, and when it finishes, it will present you with the option to activate the plugin. You should do so.

A new option will be added to your admin panel named "PowerPress." Click it. You will be given a choice between two modes: simple and advanced. Simple is good enough for 99 percent of podcasters out there, so choose it. Advanced mode provides detailed control over exactly how the information you will enter when you go to post a new podcast episode will be translated into RSS tags. You will now be asked how you want your podcast submission form to appear. Again, "simple" is an excellent choice. It will determine all the iTunes tags automatically for you based on their common sense equivalents in the default WordPress episode entry page. For example, iTunes keywords will use the "tags" field. Author will be your name in WordPress.

Click "Appearance." There is one important setting here: the archive length. In it, you will decide how many past episodes from your archive you want to make available to listeners at once. The default is ten, but you can set it to any value you like.

Finally, choose the "iTunes" option. Here you will set the keywords for your overall podcast on iTunes, its category, and its Image. You will also need to set up a new podcast on iTunes using the "Recommended Feed" given on this page. You can see the subheading "Get on iTunes" in the previous section to get advice on adding your podcast to the iTunes directory. Once you have signed up, iTunes will send you a confirmation e-mail with your podcast's location in the iTunes store. Use the address given to you in your iTunes confirmation e-mail to fill in the iTunes Subscription URL setting. It might take a few days for iTunes to send you the URL.

Adjust maximum file upload settings

By default, this version of WordPress limits uploads to only two megabytes in size or between one and three minutes of audio. This is not very good for your new podcast. Unfortunately, there is no simple interface for changing this. You will need to dive straight into the WordPress configuration files. Open a plain text editor, such as Windows Notepad. Do not use Microsoft Word, as it does not output plain text, but rather sophisticated DOC files. Open the following file:

```
C:\Program Files\wordpress-3.0.1-0\php\etc\
php.ini
```

Or, under Mac OS X:

```
/Applications/wordpress-3.0.1-0/php/etc/php.
ini
```

The numbers following "wordpress" in the file can change depending on when you download your copy of WordPress. There will be hundreds of settings listed in this text file, but you only need to adjust three of them: upload_max_size, post_max_size, and max_execution_time. Assuming you will want to post at least a few video podcasts at some time in the near future, the following should be appropriate settings:

```
upload_max_filesize = 500M
post_max_size = 505M
max_execution_time = 5000
```

This gives you up to 5000 seconds — or around an hour and a half — to complete any uploads and specifies a maximum upload and post size of just under half a gigabyte — plenty of space for even a video podcast episode of HD quality. If you feel confident you will never use video, you might decide to set these instead to a value such as 50 or 100M.

Last of all, you will need to restart your computer so that the settings will be updated, and reopen your administration panel by going to the following URL: **http://localhost:8080/wordpress/wp-adminl**.

Upload your episode

Click the "Media" tag and "Add new." Unlike in Podbean.com, in WordPress, adding your podcast is a two-step process: First, you upload your episode into the media library, and then, you create a post that links to that media file. To upload your episode, click the "Media" and "Add New" tab. Click "Select File" and choose a file to upload. Because you are "uploading" the file to another location on your own computer, the upload will occur almost instantly.

Next, click the "Library" item under the "Media" tab. Find your episode and click its "Edit" link. Find the "File URL," and highlight and copy it.

Now, click the "New Post" link at the top of the page. Most of this is self-explanatory. Put the title of the show in the "Title" box and the description in the text box. Your excerpt will be the short description that appears in iTunes, so write a few sentences about your show there as well. Write a few tags — keywords and short phrases that help search engines find your show based on topic — as well and place them in the "tags" box. Separate each tag with a comma. For example, a show on Roman Catholicism might use the tags: "Catholic, Roman Catholic, Christianity, Pope Benedict".

Finally, go to the "Media URL" and paste the file URL from the media library.

You now have a running podcast server on your own computer. You can see the RSS feed by going to **http://localhost:8080/wordpress/?feed=rss2**.

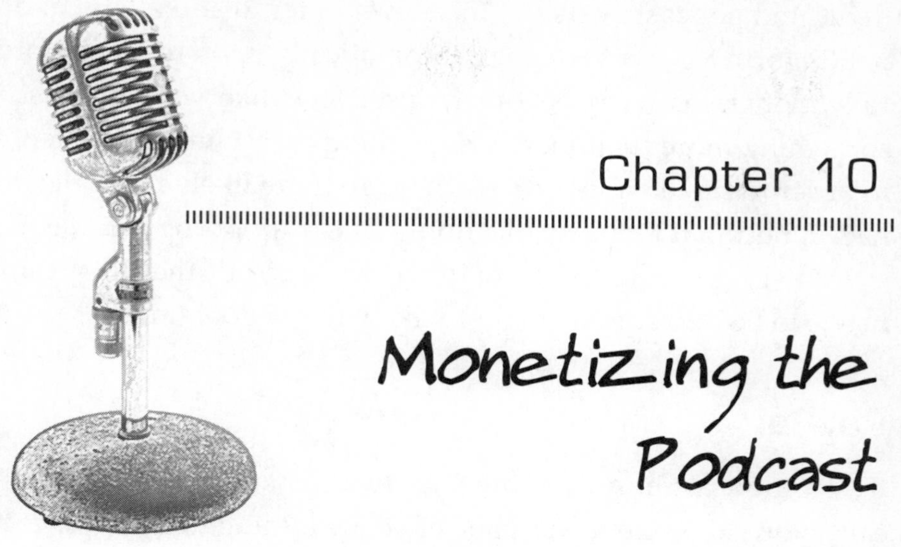

Chapter 10

Monetizing the Podcast

Many, perhaps most, podcasters produce and distribute their shows out of their own pockets for simple love of their topic. Nonetheless, it is a scarce person among us that is not excited at the thought of earning a little money on the side for doing something they love, and a few podcasters even succeed in making a living out of what they do. This chapter will cover some of the approaches podcasters use to defray their costs and even scratch out a living from their passion.

Donations

The simplest method of monetization is to simply ask for and take donations. All it requires is an account at an online money transfer service like PayPal and a Web page, which you will need in order to host the RSS file for your show anyway. Some of the dedicated podcast hosts out there even offer to add a PayPal donation form to your Web page automatically upon request. Naturally, donations work best if the user feels like your podcast is something more than merely something entertaining to listen to in order to stave off boredom. They are more likely to hit the donation button if they feel like doing so is supporting a cause. For example, if you are trying to get a message out that they think needs to be heard, you are more likely to get donations.

PayPal

If your podcast host does not supply a donations link automatically, you can achieve the same effect by adding this HTML code to the Web page for your podcast:

```
<form name="_xclick" action="https://www.
paypal.com/cgi-bin/webscrhttps://www.paypal.
com/cgi-bin/webscr" method="post">
<input type="hidden" name="cmd" value="_
xclick">
<input type="hidden" name="business"
value="me@mybusiness.comme@mybusiness.com">
<input type="hidden" name="item_name"
value="Team In Training">
<input type="hidden" name="currency_code"
value="USD">
<input type="hidden" name="amount" val-
ue="25.00">
<input type="image" src="http://www.paypal.
com/en_US/i/btn/btn_donate_LG.gifhttp://www.
paypal.com/en_US/i/btn/btn_donate_LG.gif"
```

```
border="0" name="submit" alt="Make payments
with PayPal - it's fast, free and secure!">
</form>
```

You will need to replace the "business," "item_name," and default donation "amount" to appropriate values to suit your show. For example, if your podcast name is "Stroller Cast," you want your default donation to be $5, and your PayPal account uses the -email address "producer@strollercast.com," then you should change the following lines in the form:

```
<input type="hidden" name="business"
value="producer@strollercast.com">
<input type="hidden" name="item_name"
value="Stroller Cast">
<input type="hidden" name="amount" val-
ue="5.00">
```

This code was taken from the PayPal website and is accurate as of publication time. PayPal is a stable and mature service, so changes that break the button are unlikely to occur. However, if you wish to check PayPal for alterations, you can check it yourself at **www.paypal.com/cgi-bin/webscr?cmd=_pdn_donate_techview_outside**.

PayPal's fee system can be a bit involved. When receiving a money transfer directly from a bank account or another PayPal account, the service is provided free of charge. However, when it comes from a debit or credit card, PayPal takes a small percentage, plus $.030. As of writing, the percentage was 2.9 percent, but it could change over time.

Flattr

PayPal is the easiest way to set up donation schemes and is easily the most likely to be recognized by your users, but Flattr (**http://flattr.com**), a relatively new service, is changing that. Flattr works in a fashion similar to PayPal, but it is more dedicated and streamlined for exactly the purpose of allowing visitors to donate to their favorite Web and podcast creators. Users transfer money into an account, and participating websites add a "Flattr" button to their own site. Each user determines for him or herself how much money they would like to donate, in total, to articles, videos, and podcasts during the course of that month. At the end of the month, 10 percent is taken by Flattr to support the service, and the other 90 percent is divided up amongst all the creations that the user chooses to "flattr." For example, suppose a user determines that they wish to spend $10 per month to support creators. Over the course of the month, he or she clicks the "Flattr" button on nine different items, including two of your podcast episodes. At the end of the month, the Flattr service takes $1 out of the $10 to pay the bills and distributes the other $9 to the nine flattered creations. Because your podcast got two flatters from the user, your cut would be $2. If, instead, the user had flattered 18 items, then the $9 would be divided between those.

The service is still in its infancy, so a few details are likely to change over the coming years, but there are a few major caveats to podcasters who wish to use Flattr as a tool for monetization. The first, of course, is that Flattr is designed for users that intend to donate to websites on a regular basis. Few users are likely to set up Flattr accounts for the sole purpose of making a one-time donation to your service, so it would be wise to leave a PayPal option open for users who might not donate on a regular basis.

The other is that creators are required to set up accounts as donors themselves before they can receive any donations. Lastly, the service is based in Europe, and though it handles currency conversions itself, all accounts are managed in terms of euros. The minimum monthly donation amount is two euros, or around $2.50 at the time of writing. Because creators are required to also be donors, any creator wishing to receive donations through Flattr must be willing to pony up at least two euros to support other creators of their choice. Even if a user never flatters an item, the money is taken and given to a charity of Flattr's choice.

Flattered podcasters are paid every month, provided that they receive at least ten euros worth of flatters. Otherwise, the money carries over to the next month until the total reaches at least ten.

Advertising

Donations alone can plausibly pay the hosting bills on a small- to medium-sized podcast, but they are unlikely to even come close to compensating you for the time and energy needed to support the show. If you view podcasting as a way to bring in revenue, you would probably get a better return on your investment by taking a part-time job at a fast-food restaurant. This is fine for many podcasters; they are in it as a hobby and are not looking to get much more from their donations than help in paying the server fees.

If your intentions for your podcast go beyond this, including potentially making podcasting your career, you are going to need to look for something more than charity. Advertising is the way to go. Advertising makes the media world go round. Television, radio, newspapers, magazines, and websites large and small earn a substantial portion, if not all, of their income by selling space or airtime to vendors looking to communicate with their customers.

CPM

Advertising over the Internet, including through podcasts, is usually expressed in terms of CPM, or "cost per thousand," with "M" being the Roman numeral for the number one thousand. An agreement is reached with an advertiser to pay a certain rate for every thousand impressions his or her ad receives. Rates vary a great deal for Web content, from as little as one dollar CPM — or one dollar for every thousand viewers — to as much as a hundred dollars CPM — or a hundred dollars for every thousand viewers. It is impossible to give any precise estimates for what CPM is reasonable for a given podcast. Though it is generally more than the average starting podcaster tends to believe, there are too many factors in play. Advertisers want to get their information to the people that are likely to act on that information and buy their products. So besides simple audience sizes, they also care a great deal about things like the typical income of their audience. For example, most advertisers would prefer a guaranteed 20-second spiel directly solely at billionaire Warren Buffet over the same 20 seconds directed at even a thousand minimum wage earners. One result is that, if you can show that your podcast is of interest to middle-aged professionals making over a $100,000 a year, this one fact alone can secure you a far higher CPM rate than if your podcast appealed primarily to high school students.

Some advertisers (such as Google AdWords) will not use a CPM system to determine advertising payments. They express their advertising rates in terms of eCPM, or effective cost per thousand, where the rate is translated to a CPM to make it easier for podcasters to compare rates between multiple sources.

Your advantage

As a podcaster, you have one significant advantage over most other forms of media competing for marketing budgets of those vendors. Put simply: You are hyper-specialized. Look from an advertiser's point of view. What do they care about? Counter-intuitively, what most advertisers care about is not the number of people who will be exposed to their advertisement. Instead, they care about the type of people viewing their advertisements. Unless they sell products that nearly all people use and want, they care about exposing their product to the people who will actually be interested in buying it. For example, a vendor for cross-country, high-end bicycles has two options: a show on a radio station that will reach a hundred thousand listeners or your podcast dedicated to cross-country cycling that reaches a mere thousand listeners. Who do they choose? A hundred thousand potential buyers sounds impressive, but how many are really interested in their products? In other words, how many are really potential buyers? The U.S. Census in 2000 estimated that only 0.5 pecent of Americans ride bicycles on a regular basis. According to this statistic, advertisers do not have a choice between a hundred thousand potential buyers or one thousand potential buyers. They have a choice between advertising with the radio station and getting their product mentioned to 500 potential buyers and 99,500 disinterested – and probably annoyed – listeners or advertising with your podcast and getting their message out to a thousand potential buyers who have indicated their own interest. At the beginning of the book, you read about how hyper-specialization was necessary to build a listener base. Turns out that is only a half-truth. It is not just necessary to building a listener base; it is also your key to the getting a return on the value of your podcast and its listener base.

If you ever find yourself on the phone with a potential advertiser who asks you exactly that question, remember to give them the answer: quality beats quantity. Would they rather get their message out to a hundred thousand random people who just happen to live in the neighborhood or a thousand people with an active, declared interest in exactly the product they happen to be selling? Even a modestly successful podcast with a focused, hyper-specialized topic can out perform the multi-million dollar, but generic, media outlets when it comes to returning an advertiser's investments.

Speaking of the listener base, this is your key to how you should think about your podcast when it comes time to see it as an advertisement-supported business. You are building a base of listeners and providing them with something they want, and in return, they provide you with the 15 to 20 seconds per episode that you can spend plugging a product. It should be understood that no one is going to subscribe to a podcast that consists of nothing but commercials. One study revealed that over 30 percent of Americans turn the radio off as soon as the commercials come on. One reason for that is because most of the commercials on the radio are irrelevant to them — a problem your podcast will be spared from. The same survey found that over 80 percent of listeners considered listening to commercials in exchange for a free service was a fair deal. Nonetheless, you will need something to draw your listeners to the show. They have to get something in return for that valuable 15 to 20 seconds of their time that they spend listening to commercials.

One difficult decision about advertisements is where to put them? Your advertisers want their money's worth. They will generally want to be mentioned as early in the show as possible, if not at the very beginning, and as far from other advertisements as possible. It can be tempting to give them what they want; after all, they are the ones handing over the money. However, it is the listener's time you are selling them, and potentially loyal listeners are worth far more than any single advertiser. Any time you are tempted to put an advertisement in the beginning of an episode, you might want to consider this statistic: New potential listeners will play your most recent episode and give you, at most, 30 seconds to impress them. The first 30 seconds of every single episode, from first to last, are critical. If you fail to engage the listener's interest in those 30 seconds, you have lost a potential listener, probably forever, which means you have lost all the advertising income that listener could have brought in. Given a choice between building up and expanding your base of listeners and making a fast buck, you would be better off bringing in more listeners that you can sell to advertisers later.

When you insert the advertisement into your podcast, there is generally no need to be sneaky about it. On the contrary, some podcasters report the greatest success when they explicitly refer to the advertisers as their sponsors, thank them for making the show possible, and make known to the listeners that it is the support of the advertising company "and viewers like you" that make the free delivery of the show possible. This sort of relationship also works well with something the advertisers themselves want: exclusivity.

It is not hard to see why. If you were the Clover Hill Bicycle Company trying to draw people to your service, which of the following plugs would you prefer for your bikes:

"We would like to thank the following groups and individuals for making this show possible: Stephen Lambert, Motorola, Google, Gigavox, Atlantic Press, Wordsworth Publishing, Clover Hill Bicycles, Sideshow Bob, my mother, all our viewers, and all my friends."

or

"We would like to extend our heartfelt thanks to Clover Hill Bicycle Company, whose support, along with viewers like you, has made this show possible. That's Clover Hill Bicycle, which just released its latest model: the Mountaineer. It's as rugged as it is stylish."

Naturally, Clover Hill will pay a great deal more for the second advertisement, and it does not hurt that your listeners, even the most jaded and impatient with commercials, would far and above prefer the latter advertisement to the first. Successful podcasters have found that exclusive, sponsorship-style advertisements, like the second one above, bring in more money from advertisers seeking a one-on-one talk with the potential buyers and are also more tolerable to listeners. This is particularly true when sponsorships are compared to shotgun-style advertisements that run commercials by the listener one after the other in a flurry that listeners quickly learn to tune out and skip.

Preparing a media kit

When it comes time to make phone calls to potential advertisers, you will need a media kit, a two- or three-page guide that explains to advertising executives what your podcast is, who listens to it, and why it would be in their best interest to sponsor your show. Advertisers will expect you to be able to produce this information on demand, so you should have it ready before you even talk to the first advertiser. Two pieces of information will be paramount in its production: your demographics and your rates, along with what, precisely, they get for their money.

Compiling demographics is the easier of the two. Websites such as SurveyMonkey (**www.surveymonkey.com**) and Zoomerang (**www.zoomerang.com**) sell formal surveying services for podcasters, and you can present the survey to your customers as a chance to "make themselves heard." You should ask five to ten questions that you think will get at the information your advertisers will care about, and a few common questions inquire about your listeners' level of education, income, age, gender, and how often they buy products related to the podcast topic. Advertisers like to know this information because they already have a picture in their heads of what their customers look like in these terms, and a vendor will appreciate knowing that it is paying to reach listeners who have the financial resources to act on their impulses and not merely the interest. However, do not be content with only generic questions like these. Advertisers want to know this data because they are familiar with it, but that is only because they are used to dealing with generic, big media outlets that cannot be any more specific. Your greatest asset is your narrow focus. Use your survey as a way to show your narrow focus to your advertisers. If you run a cycling podcast, let your advertisers know that 90 percent of your listeners are in the bike shops with money to spend at least once a year. If your podcast is about horror books, let your advertisers know that 90 percent of your listeners buy at least one horror novel a month and that a similar percentage value your advice on books "highly or very highly."

Choosing rates is a harder proposition. Most of your listeners are only too happy to sound off at the slightest provocation, but few of your advertisers are going to sit down and tell you the highest price they would pay for a given type of advertisement. It is going to take some experimentation to arrive at the best rates for your show, but in general, the rates are higher than what many podcasters believe. Most podcasters, looking at their show, compare them to the big media companies, and believe that because they have low overhead, their advertising rates must be pretty low also. However, this is generally not true. Your advertisers want to know how many listeners you have and what sort of people they are, and they will pay handsomely to get to the right folks — the ones most likely to be influenced by the ad to at least consider their product. They do not particularly care what your overhead is, and it only takes a few thousand targeted listeners to make the advertiser interested.

Advertisers want exclusivity, so you do not need a lot of advertisers. If you set up a sponsorship system, where each advertiser gets credit for sponsoring exactly one show, it will be easy to find the right rates. As soon as your first advertiser bites, you are in the right ballpark, especially if he or she comes back for more. Once you have a basic rate figured out, you can experiment by offering other options and changing what an advertiser gets for that rate. A successful podcast will bring in anywhere from $40 to $100 CPM, or $40 to $100 per thousand downloads in sponsorships.

Later in this chapter, there will be a section on affiliate programs in greater detail. However, this is a good place to mention that these programs are a great source of early "sponsors." They spare you the sales calls, give you a solid bottom line for what your advertising spots are worth, and give you some time to build a user base and gather information on your listener demographics. The idea is simple: After becoming associated with an affiliate program for a product, in which you receive a commission for all sales of the product that come back to your website or podcast, you simply tell your listeners that the show is sponsored by that product and give them the affiliate track-back link or another link that redirects to it.

Listener intimacy and endorsements

It has been said before, but podcasting is an intimate medium. Your listeners are going to develop a sense that they know you and value your take, whatever is. Anything you can do to encourage that is important. Your credibility is very important. The video gaming Web-based comic strip Penny Arcade, which has since become a podcast, a series of video games, and a successful blog, has that experience. As it began to transition their popular website from a hobby and into a source revenue, it saw its credibility as a valuable asset. It was able to tell its listeners, with a straight face, that a product was good or bad, and that any advertised product really was worthy of its endorsement. In short, it took its own endorsement seriously, and that while that might make for fewer potential advertisers for them, this credibility and trust means that potential advertisers are willing to pay more to have Tycho and Gabe say, "This is an awesome game." Of course, your advertisers would be pleased with this bit of info as well.

They would much rather receive an endorsement from a person whose listeners see him or her as a straight-shooter than a sell-out.

Ad Networks and Affiliate Programs

Most people are familiar with Google AdSense or at least have seen the Google AdSense advertisements. These little boxes analyze the contents of a website and attempt to make a guess, based on common words, about what sort of advertisements viewers are likely to want. Some webmasters make thousands of dollars per month off this system of advertisements, but most find the ads scarcely worth the time, bringing in only pennies. Similar networks exist for podcasts, inserting advertisements automatically into the show. Overall, ad networks are not the way to go if you want your podcast to bring in optimal revenue. Even the most modest sponsorship campaigns will bring in around $40 CPM, while few ad network programs succeed in paying more a few dollars CPM. You will be better off with direct corporate sponsorship or even affiliate programs than ad networks, but they are popular for a reason. Sales-shy webmasters, podcasters, and other creators can set up an account and insert advertisements into their programs in minutes, with almost no effort or technical expertise. The ad networks handle all the sales and link tracking, and all the creators have to do is cash the check. The only flaw is that the check will be unlikely to pay even the hosting costs. At most, ad networks should be no more than a small part of your plans for revenue, and a temporary one at that, until a more profitable affiliate or sponsorship system can be set up.

Affiliate programs abandon the CPM model, though you generally still can (and should) think of them in CPM terms. Rather than an advertiser paying you a set fee for a number of episode downloads, you give your listeners promo codes or tracking URLs where they can go to purchase the vendors product, and you earn a commission for every purchase your listeners make. This spreads the risk a little more evenly between the podcaster and the advertiser. The podcaster who can deliver the goods to his or her advertiser is paid, and the advertiser can rest assured that he or she will not pay premium advertising rates in advance for a lackluster, one-second mention at the end of the show. Keep in mind that, if you choose the affiliate program, your success or failure will depend greatly on your credibility to your listeners. If a listener spends cash on a bad product because you suggested it, you are only destroying your own business model. On the other hand, direct your listeners to the good stuff, and they will take your word seriously in future buying decisions.

Blubrry

Blubrry (**www.blubrry.com**) is a podcast host, ad networking, and affiliate program. The hosting and advertising services are not connected, so you can participate in the free ad network and affiliate programs without getting your hosting through Blubrry. This leaves you free to shop around and use any hosting service you like. By signing up for the program, Blubrry connects you with a variety of advertising opportunities that you are free to accept or decline. Some opportunities are available only for specific groups of podcasts, while others are available to all. The best deals are paid in terms of CPM, while most of the starting deals are affiliate programs that pay a commission. Once you have signed an advertising deal, most of the contracts on Blubrry leave its implementation to you. They expect a verbal plug from the host at some point in the show and include promo codes or track-back links that the host can give out to obtain a commission, which usually offer the listener a discount. Signing up is easy; you need a valid podcast feed URL and an entry in the iTunes store to get started. Narrated video screencasts are provided on the Blubrry website to help you get the process started.

Whether you like Blubrry depends on how comfortable you feel giving a plug for a product yourself. This gives you more freedom. Most of the programs leave you a wide leeway to determine which aspect of their service you choose to plug and how you approach the topic with your listeners. Of course, it is in your best interest to make your plug in a prominent place in the show that your listeners are likely to hear and in a way to which they will respond. For example, though they suggest mentioning the product in the first tenth of the show, the final decision is left up to you. If you feel comfortable speaking to your listeners directly and asking them to support you by supporting your sponsor, Blubrry can be a good deal. However, if you would rather distance yourself a little more from your advertisements, another network might be a better choice.

VoloMedia

With VoloMedia (www.volomedia.com), in order to get the highest paying contracts, which track media plays even on offline iPods or other MP3 players, all of your listeners are required to install plugin software on their own computers. That is a pretty big limitation, but it is only required for the best contracts. A lower paying "network service" is available for podcasters that are uncomfortable asking their listeners to install third-party software.

ClickBank (**www.clickbank.com**) is a large affiliate network that allows you to browse thousands of products that offer a commission to podcasters, Web masters, and anyone else who can help bring in sales. The service works primarily as a matchmaker, and it is your responsibility to find products you would like to try to sell, which can be a bit time consuming. Many of the products on the site are less than thrilling, and you will need a few hours to wade through the junk to find something you feel comfortable recommending to your listeners.

Amazon Associates

If you have seen small Amazon.com banner ads on your favorite blogs or podcasting websites, representing what the author is currently reading or which book he or she suggests for the audience, chances are that blogger or podcaster is member of the Amazon Associates program — an affiliate network that provides Web content creators with up to a 15 percent commission on sales of books and other goods that can be traced back to their websites. If you can find content on Amazon that suites your podcast subject matter, participating in the Amazon Associates program can be an excellent way to earn cash. Your listeners are unlikely to appreciate a hard sell, but they will quite likely thank you if you direct them toward some of the books, movies, and products that you have found helpful and informative for your show.

Direct Sales

Advertising and affiliate programs are the most common method that professional podcast producers, just like other media producers, use to earn revenue for their podcast; however, they are not the only route open to you. You can also supplement your income by selling products directly to your listeners. Successful direct sales programs have sold their listeners everything from best of compilations to T-shirts and coffee mugs.

Walking billboards, CafePress, and cash

The simplest way to implement a direct sales program is to open an account at CafePress (**www.cafepress.com**), the on-demand manufacturer of custom t-shirts, coffee mugs, and bumper stickers. Using their system, you can have an online store open in only a few minutes. You even set the prices, provided you charge at least as much as CafePress charges you per item. For example, CafePress may take the first $15 of a shirt, and you can set the price to anything higher than that to determine your payout. Do not let the ease of opening a store fool you; CafePress makes little to no effort to market your goods. You will still need to build a base of loyal listeners who not only enjoy your show and tune in to listen regularly but who are excited at the prospect of paying twenty bucks for the privilege of wearing your logo. Naturally, this works best if you have either a creative show people can be excited about, or you advocate for a cause that listeners will want to let the world know they support. It does not hurt to have a little talent in Adobe Photoshop either, as the design is left entirely to you.

Subscriptions

Like magazines or cable television stations, a few podcasts charge their listeners a monthly or yearly fee for access to the show. Few podcasts survive using a subscription-based system, though there are some major exceptions. MagnaTunes, for one, distributes a series of free podcasts containing music in a variety of formats. All the music is licensed under the Creative Commons license, which allows users to download and share the music free, but MagnaTunes appeals to listeners to purchase the music or pay a $15 a per month fee to support the artists and receive access to a longer, commercial-free version of the podcast and a larger archive. This is generally how such subscription services must work to survive; the listeners do not so much buy the current episodes, but they buy the right to download older and or missed episodes or to download a special, commercial-free version of the show.

"Best of" sets

Mature podcasts with a large library of past shows might also see some benefit in selling "best of" sets, which can be a CD, DVD, or digital copy of the best or most popular episodes from the show's past, usually episodes that have long been removed from the RSS feed. This can be a particularly effective method if you find yourself getting e-mails or comments from listeners who want to hear an older favorite show. A variation would be to package a full CD or DVD with the entire show's history as bonus for "completists" in your audience. It is usually best to throw in something new along with the set, as well. Dedicated, long-time fans who might not pay for a CD set of shows that they have already heard will sometimes fork over their credit cards for a few bonus episodes only available to purchasers of the set.

CASE STUDY: A SUCCESSFULLY MONETIZED PODCAST

Jeff McQuillan, Ph.D., creator and host
ESL Pod
Center for Educational Development, Inc.
PO Box 66577, Los Angeles, CA 90066
www.eslpod.com * eslpod@eslpod.com

Dr. Jeff McQuillan and his co-host Dr. Lucy Tse are both former professors of applied linguistics and education and have taught English as a second language (ESL) at a number of grade levels. Together, they saw podcasting as a way to teach the subject they love without having to deal with what McQuillan calls the "traditional gatekeepers of the education publishing world." At first, it was a hobby. They wanted to give foreign students interested in learning English a free resource for doing so. They still give away most of the content produced for the podcast, but some resources are sold, so that McQuillan and Tse can afford to work full time on the show.

They publish three episodes a week, and though they keep their listener numbers secret, they have regularly been featured as one of the most popular education podcasts on iTunes. To get the word out, they have counted primarily on iTunes and word of mouth.

McQuillan estimates that, between himself and his colleague, each episode requires around ten hours of preparation. To pay the bills, they sell subscriptions to a "learning guide" for each episode, along with a series of stand-alone courses.

His advice for new podcasters: Podcasting is a very intimate, personal medium. Your listeners can tell if you are trustworthy and sincere, so be straight with them. It is not just about the content. It is about the relationship between you and your listeners.

RSS Perks

Despite the ease of use and prevalence of podcatchers like iTunes, a substantial number of listeners, over 60 percent, prefer to listen to and watch podcasts directly through their Web browsers. As a podcast producer, you want to ensure your audience is able to consume your show in whatever format they prefer, whether they want to listen on portable audio devices, podcatchers, or Web browsers. However, it is in your best interest to lean a little bit on the Web browser crowd to take advantage of the benefits of RSS syndication. Put simply, users left to manually navigate to your content are more likely to stop checking in after a short time for more shows. Of course, it is one thing if a user decides they are no longer interested in what you produce; you cannot please everyone all the time, after all. Some people naturally are going to become interested and then fade away or only want to watch one episode on a topic of particular interest to them. That is natural. However, it is quite another thing to set a listener on fire, bring him or her in, get him or her interested, and lose him or her forever simply because he or she forgot your Web address. You do not want that to happen and, really, neither does your listener. While continuing to make the show as easy to access as possible, it is worth considering giving your RSS listeners a few perks. For example, occasionally, you might want to post a single show to your RSS feed, and, rather than post it immediately to your show's website, post a notification that a show has been posted that is only available to subscribers. Make sure you let them know that the subscription is free and allows listeners to keep up with the latest episodes of all their favorite podcasts automatically.

Chapter 11

Marketing Your Podcast

Now that you have your podcast recorded and published, it is time to start thinking about how you will market it. Depending upon your personality, this is either the bread and butter of what you are getting into podcasting for or you are highly tempted to skip this chapter. Those in the former camp do not need a sales pitch on the virtues of sparing some thought and effort on how they intend to let people know about their show's existence. You can skip the next few paragraphs. However, if the thought of marketing your show makes your skin crawl, you are not alone. Most podcasters make their show, upload it to their server, and never go a step further to market their show than to let the iTunes directory know about its existence. If that is what you want, let the next a few sentences attempt to dissuade you. Marketing your show does not mean sacrificing content to the soulless vagaries of keyword optimization. By failing to market your podcast, you are missing a lot of what podcasting is about and what separates it from traditional media. Podcasting, as opposed to radio and television, is a form of social media. You are going to find yourself in a community — not just with your listeners, but with the other podcasters, Web hosts, and bloggers in your topic as well. If you do not want to put time and thought into marketing your show, the image you probably have of what it would be like and feel like to go that route could be summed up in a photograph of a used car salesman with slicked-back hair named "Honest Al." However, not putting any thought into marketing is more like being the guy who sits in the back of the bar, at a table by himself. Your potential listeners are your potential community, even your potential friends. And just like in real life, sometimes you are the one who has to take the initiative.

SEO

Search engine optimization (SEO) has found itself with a tawdry reputation. To some degree, that reputation is deserved. We have all, at least a few times, went to the all-knowing Google to search for some needed bit of information or amusement and found ourselves staring at a useless page, stuffed with keywords. An entire industry seems to have sprung up to analyze every stray search query in the hopes of finding the magic keywords that will funnel eyes and ears straight to high-paying advertisements.

However, this is no reason to write SEO off entirely. It is a perfectly legitimate and necessary enterprise in which to invest some time for finding ways to ensure that the people who want your content can find it as quickly and easily as possible. SEO is only bad when it is used as a trick to drive traffic to useless content. If you are providing a show people want to watch or listen to, then time invested in making sure that the people find it is far from being a seedy manipulation of the search engines. Rather, it is a service to the Internet and even the search engines themselves, which exist primarily as a service to help searchers find what they want. The fact that it can expand our listenership, making our own podcast more successful and maybe even more profitable, does not hurt either.

Text driven SEO

A podcaster who wishes to optimize for SEO faces a dilemma. Though there are a few experimental search engines out there that analyze audio and video data itself to provide search results, they will not be viable for consumers for a few years. For now and for the foreseeable future, text-driven, keyword-based search is king, which means a podcaster must go a little further out of his or her way to make his or her content visible to the search engines for analysis. Simply posting episodes with a title and a short, paragraph description will make the podcaster's RSS feed and home page appear to search engines like Google and Yahoo! as very shallow content. Whereas competitors with text-based pages will have entire articles sprinkled with keywords, all your content is locked inside an audio or video file where search engines cannot find it. Wayne Lin, founder of the SEO consultant firm Wayne Write Productions, could not put this fact any better. He says the key to SEO is transparency to the search engines. If the engines do not have text to analyze, any further SEO practices are worthless.

There are a few steps you can take to alleviate this problem, and while they can be labor intensive (especially if you do not choose to fully script your shows in advance), they can even fit into your podcast's website as an organic and listener-appreciated features. The first solution is to have a transcript for every episode and the second is to have show notes.

CASE STUDY: AN SEO EXPERT ON PODCASTS

Wayne Lin, founder and SEO expert
Wayne Write Productions
waynelin1981@gmail.com
Phone: (405) 514-7882

Wayne Lin is the founder of the SEO consulting start-up Wayne Write Productions. He started out as a freelance writer building his portfolio when he answered an advert for SEO writers. Since then, SEO has been his bread and butter, and he works full time on helping webmasters, bloggers, and podcasters optimize their websites for the best possible search engine results. He offers a few bits of advice for podcasters looking to optimize their podcast website for the search engines:

First, create content for the user, not the search engine. The key to SEO is search engine transparency — making sure the search engines can easily read your content. At the same time, remember that the search engines function based on text and keywords.

Next, stay away from black hat SEO. The search engines make certain that the penalties for dishonest SEO practices are always higher than the benefits.

Finally, establish credibility. One of the key things the search engines are trying to find is your credibility on the Internet. Blog regularly and consistently. Strive to have unique content.

Transcript

When you post your show, ensure that you provide a link to another page on your site that contains a full transcript of the show. For some listeners, this is a useful idea. Some listeners like to read as they listen, in order to have an easy way to check what was said about a topic without rewinding the playback or simply to access your content in situations where headphones or speakers would be inappropriate, such as during a coffee break at work. It is safe to say that most listeners will probably only rarely check the transcripts, but Web crawlers used by the search engines to examine the content of the Internet will consume them readily. With a full show transcript, your podcast closes the visibility gap with more traditional text-based websites. But, unlike recording the show, they are not exactly fun to produce.

The simplest way to get a transcript is to write it in advance as a script, record the show, following the script more or less, and then post the script with the show as an added feature. The most difficult, frustrating path is to sit down and listen to the show, typing what you hear. There is no need to get a certification in court reporting, though. If you prefer not to script, the best way is to invest in quality speech recognition software, a special computer program that takes an audio recording of a person speaking and attempts to translate the recorded speech into a text file. "Attempts" is the keyword here. Most speech recognition programs will make mistakes, sometimes quite drastic mistakes, at least once or twice every few sentences. Nonetheless, correcting the mistakes is far faster than attempting to type out regular podcast episodes manually. If you own Windows Vista or 7, it comes with a powerful engine built into the accessibility options. If you do not, there are still other options. Popular software includes Dragon Naturally Speaking for the PC and MacSpeech for the Mac. However, these come with fairly hefty price tags. Prices start around $100 for the home editions and climb to approximately $600 for professional packages. There are two free speech recognition engines: Simon (**http://simon-listens.org**) and Carnegie

Mellon University's Sphinx software (**http://cmusphinx.sourceforge.net**). The CMU Sphinx program is primarily designed for academics and researchers, so it can be a very difficult tool to use.

Show notes

Show Notes can be a useful tool to feed the search engines the text they need and engage listeners. Rather than provide a link to a full transcript of an entire episode, you invite listeners to go to your website to see the show notes for each episode. These text pages, anywhere from a few to dozens of pages long, are a good choice. If transcripts feel like overkill, however, they can be useful even in addition to transcripts. You can use them to go into greater depth on topics you covered, provide HTML links to resources that readers might be interested in, and even include simple Web polls and comment functions for the listeners to make themselves heard.

Keywords in the title

A common mistake many podcasters make is to think only of the "tags" or "keywords" section of their posts as existing for the search engines. Many podcasters compose their descriptions and even their episode titles with no thought of all toward how Google's bots will see them. The truth is, Google inspects every bit of text it can find to determine the value of the page, and it usually is not impressed when a user provides dozens of keywords and tags for the search engine that never, or only very rarely, appear elsewhere on the page. Wherever they can fit organically on the page, use the keywords for your episode, especially in prominent places such as titles. Google bots even examine the fonts on websites to find headings and topics and gives them special weight. At the very minimum, you should know what your keywords are and ensure that they occur, at the very minimum, somewhere in your domain name and title of each podcast episode. Put some thought into it. If you discover that your audience is far more likely to search for "car" than "automobile," use "car" rather than "automobile" whenever organically possible.

An important caveat is the word "organically." In the days of the early Internet, search engines could be fooled into producing massive amounts of traffic for a page by a transparent technique known as "keyword stuffing," which involves filling an entire page with nothing but hundreds upon hundreds of carefully selected keywords. Keyword stuffing rarely works now. Pages that use keywords in a suspicious way are flagged and punished by the search engines with abysmally poor results. More than one dabbling website creator has picked up some out of date advice on SEO, stuffed a website full of irrelevant (but popular keywords), and found him or herself shoved down from a modest position on the first or second page of the Google results to a far more abysmal position on the tenth or 15th page. Rather than try to implement a naive and most likely counter-productive keyword stuffing campaign, use tools like the Google Insights and Google Analytics.

The simpler of the two is Google Insights. Users can simply plug in multiple alternative keywords for a podcast episode to see which one is the most likely to garner search results. For example, a podcaster doing an episode on the Edwardian English writer Gilbert Keith Chesterton might be curious to know whether he should be referred to as "Gilbert Keith Chesterton," "GK Chesterton," "G.K. Chesterton," or simply "Chesterton." Plugging each alternative permutation into Google Insights is informative. Though precise numbers are not given, the most common search term is the shortest: Chesterton. However, both the full name (Gilbert Keith Chesterton) and the name with initials and without periods between the letters (GK Chesterton) are outdone fairly dramatically by "G.K. Chesterton." As a helpful bonus, popular similar searches are given as well, such as "GK Chesterton quotes."

Google Analytics is more involved and requires you to add a segment of JavaScript to your home page, but it provides essential information on who visits your website, which website they came from, and which search terms got them there. It can even use a variety of measures, such as how long the visitor remained on each page of your site, to determine whether the user found what they wanted and how they left.

Evergreen

Whenever possible, you should focus on creating content that is evergreen, which is content that will still be drawing interest months or years from now. Do not misunderstand: If your podcast is a meant to be about current events and other topics of short-term appeal, you should not sacrifice your vision to the evergreen content principle. However, if you want your episodes to reach the most ears and eyes possible, it makes sense to script the show so that knowledge about needlessly topical information is not assumed. Remember, your podcast episodes will likely be around and listened to for months — if not years — after you record them. The popular idea of the week might be completely forgotten when a listener discovers your podcast and begins working his or her way through the archives months later.

From an SEO point of view, there is a further reason to prefer evergreen content. Unless you produce podcasts for well-known news sites, it might take days or even weeks for search engines to recognize the changes after the new episode goes online. If the episode is about a topic that is out of date and of interest for only a few days or a week, you will never benefit from the initial rush that comes with the topic's short-term popularity. By the time your episode is recognized by the search engines, the moment has passed.

Page Ranks

If you stopped reading here, you would be left with the impression that search engines analyze the text on the page, with a special emphasis on titles, headings, and keywords, and simply try to match the results to the text on the page. Actually, it is not that simple. A search can produce thousands or even millions of matching websites, and something has to determine the order of the search results. To do this, the concept of a page rank is used, which ranks the pages, on a numerical scale, from one to ten based on their perceived importance and authority. Pages with a rank of ten are seen as some of the most authoritative pages on the Internet. They include Google itself, the World Wide Web Consortium, and CNN.com, along with a few dozen others. Should a given search have matches on both a page rank ten site like CNN.com and a site with a lower page rank, the page rank ten site will always come out on top.

On the other end of the spectrum is page rank zero, which is reserved solely for sites that are being penalized by Google for unscrupulous SEO practices. These include participating in schemes to increase the number of incoming links from other sites to stuffing keywords into hidden text. Hidden text is an area of a website designed to blend in with the background of the page and hide the keyword stuffing from all but the bots. Put simply, if Google catches anything that appears to be an attempt to dishonestly manipulate its results, it will penalize you.

Factors used to compute the page rank

The most important factor used to determine your page rank is backlinks, or how many and what type of sites link to yours. For example, if you are linked to by a page with a high page rank, this will have a dramatically positive influence on your page rank, and the more often you are linked to by authoritative pages, the more beneficial the boost to your own rank. The reverse is also true. Search engines maintain a "bad neighborhood" list, filled primarily with websites that are known to participate in shady SEO deals like link exchanges. Being linked to by a website in one of these "bad neighborhoods" can have a disastrous effect on PageRank.

Another possible factor that can be used to determine the PageRank is the uniqueness of the content. In particular, duplicate content warnings can be set off by long stretches of text on multiple pages that serve as exact, or extremely close, duplicates of the other text on the same or a similar site. While not disastrous, when duplicate content is discovered, the programs that compile search results quickly attempt to make a determination of which content is the original, and all other copies are flagged as "supplemental," assuring that they receive a lower rank than the original in search results.

Getting links

The best way to get the back links that are used by search engines like Google to determine the value of your podcast's website is to earn them. Produce content that other people find exciting and choose to talk about on their own blogs, podcasts, and websites. That said, you can be a little proactive in getting links.

Primarily, participate in the online communities that already exist for your topic. Most blogs allow you to post comments with a URL attached back to your home page. Take advantage of that feature whenever reasonable. Besides having a link directing back to your show's website for other visitors to see, the search engine will see a link to your own site from the original. However, no one appreciates spam, and the search engines are on the look out for posts that look like spam and are ready to penalize those who do it. Nevertheless, do not hesitate to say, in a friendly community, that you have done an episode on the topic and invite people to go have a listen.

Paid Advertising

Every podcaster should devote at least a little time to thinking of his or her show from an SEO standpoint. It is free, and the search engines want to direct users to quality content anyway. Everyone wins if you help the search engines along. However, SEO is not the only way to draw listeners to your podcast. What SEO tries to do through subtlety and study, advertising does with money.

Search engine marketing

It can take months or even years of focused effort in SEO to find yourself at the top of Google's search results for a commonly sought set of keywords, and it is usually only a passing moment. Rather than undertake such an enterprise, you might find advertising a more cost effective route. Google allows businesses to bid on the top three results of a chosen search, within a clearly disclaimed "sponsor" box. This is called Google AdWords — not to be confused with the Google AdSense ad network, which is where businesses and individuals bid for specific keyword searches that users might perform on Google's search engine. Unlike most Web advertisements, payments are made on a pay per click instance (PPC), rather than a cost per thousand (CPM) basis. You pay nothing if a user sees your link in Google's sponsored area but neglects to click on it. You only pay for every user who actually follows up and visits the page for your podcast using the sponsored link. The rates are competitive. Uncommon keywords might cost only a fraction of a cent for every user that follows the link to your website, while more common — and fiercely desired — keywords might cost as much a dollar or more per click. Whatever keywords you choose, you set your own budget when you set up your AdWords account. Tell Google that you are not interested in spending more than $10 per month, and Google will display your ads until you receive that ten dollars worth of advertising. This prevents the potentially disastrous advertising campaign that is too successful — driving tens of thousands of visitors to the site while bankrupting the podcaster. You never have to pay more than you have budgeted on AdWords. Some Web hosts even offer AdWords credit as an incentive for signing up for their service, so be sure to check the fine print when you sign up for your hosting service. It might come with as much as a hundred dollars in free advertising for your podcast.

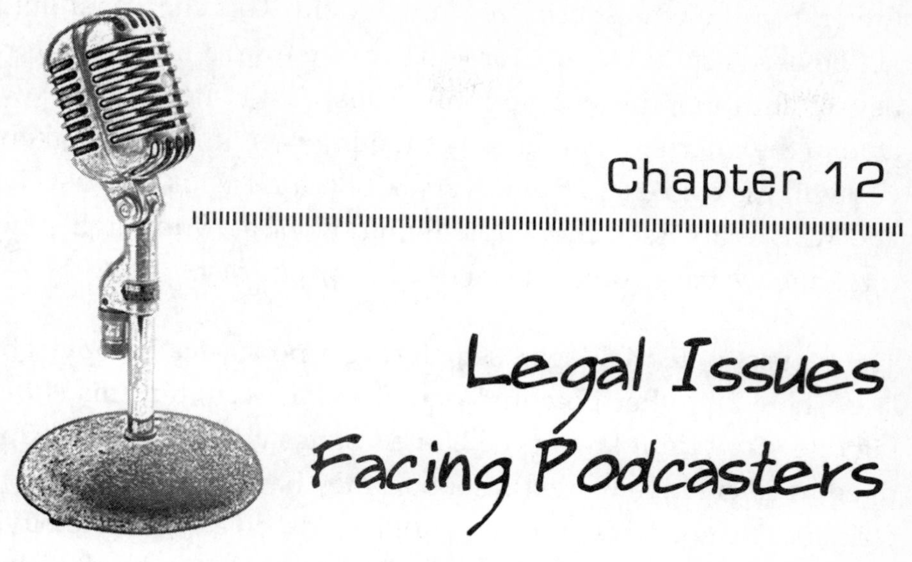

Chapter 12

Legal Issues Facing Podcasters

The technical side of podcasting is only part of the picture. Besides worrying about codecs, bit-rates, and noise floors, there are some legal issues you will need to be aware of, preferably before your podcast goes live. Mistakes here can cost a podcaster far more than all the other equipment combined.

Making the Lawyers Happy

Before going much further, this chapter is intended for informational use only. A time might come when you need to make legal decisions about your podcast. For example, you might not be 100 percent sure whether you can use a copyrighted image under the fair use doctrine, which will be discussed later in the chapter. When that time comes, you will need to consult a licensed lawyer, preferably one who specializes in that field. This chapter should not be used as a substitute for legal advice from a licensed attorney. In addition, this chapter only deals with issues of U.S. law. Due to the international nature of the Internet, it is highly likely you will have listeners from overseas. Because your podcast can and will be accessed by people living overseas, you might find foreign laws have some relevance to your podcast.

The biggest potential legal issue facing a podcaster is copyright law. There are other potential minefields as well, but this is the big one. Copyright law in the United States is automatically applied to all creative works as soon as they have been recorded or written. The good news: You do not have to do anything to have your podcast protected by U.S. copyright law. As soon as you hit the record button, copyright enters effect and remains in effect for your entire life plus 70 years after your death. The flip side of that coin is that nearly every bit of writing, art, music, or film you encounter should be assumed to be under the protection of copyright law.

What specifically does copyright law do? At the simplest level, it gives the creator of the work — or the publisher — the right to control how his or her work is used and, more specifically, whether and when copies and modifications can be made to the work. Most likely, as a podcast producer, you will not care if copies are made of your podcast episodes. After all, you will be offering them for download to anyone who wants them, but you should be happy to know that people cannot take bits of your work and reproduce them for their own ends without paying you for the trouble. However, with that protection comes the responsibility to follow the same rules. It does not matter how much you love the song "Jessie's Girl" by Rick Springfield; if you want to use it during your podcast, Springfield will expect you to ask his permission first, and most likely, he will expect a check in the mail for the trouble. Also, he always has the right to simply say "No." It is his song, after all. There are some exceptions to copyright law, however. The most notable exception to copyright law is the public domain.

Public Domain

The public domain is a term that refers to works that are not, in any way, under copyright protection. There are a number of ways something can enter the public domain:

- **Material that once enjoyed a copyright, but the copyright has since expired.** An example of this would be the writings of 19th century American writer Mark Twain.

- **Underlying ideas as distinct from their expression.** For example, the Stephen King novel *The Stand* enjoys copyright protection, but there is no protection for the idea "post-apocalyptic horror story with religious overtones."

- **Facts.** Facts enjoy no copyright protection at all; although, the expression of those facts might be protected. For example, an archaeologist named Indiana Jones discovers the remains of a lost civilization and writes a book about it. The text of the book enjoys copyright, but the facts, such as where the location was located, which tools the civilization used, and their religious beliefs are all public domain.

- **Government works.** Studies, papers, and information published by the U.S. government never enjoy copyright protection.

- **Titles and slogans.** Titles like *Indiana Jones and the Temple of Doom* and slogans like "Brighten your day with sparkle!" are a special case. They do not enjoy copyright protection, but they will most likely enjoy trademark protection, covered later this chapter.

A work in the public domain might enjoy the protection of moral rights if the creator still lives. These rights give the creator the right to insist that they be given credit for having created the work and to spare the work from alterations, particularly if those alternations could damage the reputation of the author. They usually pass away when the creator dies. They are also much stricter in many other countries than they are in the United States.

Fair Use

The fair use doctrine stipulates certain circumstances in which a person might legitimately copy a material protected by the copyright laws without getting special permission from the owner. It ought to be said that fair use has become something of a minefield. The doctrine was originally laid out in order to offer reporters, critics, and researchers some peace of mind if they were to use one or two stray sentences from a novel in a review or an article about that novel. However, many, either through ignorance or malfeasance, have attempted to claim fair use protection for even patently offending violations of the copyright law only to discover that it is not as liberally applied as they had thought.

A particularly notorious example was the claim by users of the original Napster, while it was still a piracy service, that their activities were a fair use, provided they deleted the copies relatively quickly. There are no hard and fast rules that can dictate, with scientific precision, whether a copier has fair use on his or her side. It is left for the courts to decide on a case-by-case basis. In general, the courts use four basic principles in their determination of whether a given act is a fair use or not:

- **The degree of creativity that went into the copyrighted work.** It will be much harder to justify the fair use in copying a passage from a novel compared to a passage from a mathematics textbook.

- **The character of your use.** Are you merely copying the work, or is your copying transforming the original work in some way into some other work? An example of this might be music remixes that only use one or two notes from another song.

- **The amount of the work in use.** This works two ways: How much of the original work did you take, and how substantial is it compared to your resulting work? Did you copy a five-second portion of "Jessie's Girl" because you wanted it as background music for the opening of your podcast, or did you copy it because you wanted to compare it with five-second portions of other 80s pop music? The latter is more likely to be viewed as fair use because it forms a less substantial portion of the resulting podcast.

- **The potential of your work to displace the original.** Using a few bars of "Jessie's Girl" is one thing, but put most of the song in, or just the full chorus, and tech-savvy individuals may just decide to open their own copies of GarageBand and make their own MP3 of the song rather than pay Rick Springfield the $0.90 for the MP3. Be careful about something that could be considered the "heart" of the work, like the chorus of a popular song.

The courts are not limited to these factors, and none of them in isolation is sufficient to warrant a total assurance of fair use. For example, a mathematics book might be relatively uncreative compared to a novel, fulfilling the first criteria of fair use, but wholesale copying of entire chapters will never pass, no matter how stale and functional its prose. They are free to consider any factors they think relevant. For example, some judges may add "good faith" to the list of factors. The judge or jury might look favorably on the "good faith" shown if an individual making a fair use defense took the time to attribute the work to its original author. This is no magic weapon against a criminal or civil charge of copyright infringement, but it might tip the scales in a borderline case. More so than any other aspect of this chapter, however, it is worth emphasizing here that a podcast producer should never assume they have the right to use a work under the fair use doctrine until they have spoken with a lawyer. Fair use is a fluid and subjective area of the law, and many podcasters, especially hobbyists, have a knack for simply assuming that anything they do with a copyrighted work is fair use and discovering the hard way that it is not.

Satire and Parody

Flight of the Conchords, Weird Al Yankovic, and South Park are popular examples of the genres of satire and parody, and the genre has found a great deal of popularity in the podcast community. Podcasts like *Bell's in the Batfry* and *Onion Radio News* use parody and satire to entertain their audiences and emphasize a point. An entirely new subgenre has even appeared called machinima, which uses video game art and 3D engines to produce stories that make fun of the games in question. Though most people will use the words satire and parody interchangeably, U.S. copyright law makes a distinction between the two types of work, especially if a creator has to defend his or her actions in court as fair use. In the context of fair use, a parody is created when the podcaster takes copyrighted material from a source to make jokes about the same source.

The single most famous example of parody would be the works of Weird Al Yankovic, who takes songs like Michael Jackson's *Bad* and alters the lyrics to produce a song called *Fat*. On the other hand, a satire is created when the podcaster takes copyrighted material in order to mock another work or even just society in general. A popular instance of satire in the podcast world is *Anime Hell*, which splices short segments of Japanese cartoons, or anime, in order to mock anime fan culture overall.

In general, parody is far more likely to be seen as a fair use of copyrighted material then satire. For example, a podcaster who uses remixed clips of songs by musician and songwriter Eminem to mock the music of Eminem is more likely to be found innocent of copyright violations than one who uses the same clips to mock rap music in general. However, like all matters concerning fair use, the final decision over whether a given use is fair or in violation of the copyright law is left to a judge and will depend on how the judge sees your work in light of the four main factors.

Fair Use Cases Relevant to Podcasters

There have yet to be any major court cases in the United States involving podcasters and the fair use defense, so guidance on fair use issues must be sought from existing cases in other broadcast fields. The following cases were selected to give an overview of fair use in some situations likely in the life of a podcast. If the courts seem to reach contradictory conclusions in different cases, this only serves to emphasize the importance of consulting a qualified attorney before assuming fair use of a copyrighted work in your podcast or finding a substitute not under copyright protection.

Video-Cinema Films, Inc. v. Lloyd E. Rigler. Roughly a minute and half of video was taken from a five-minute opera performance and broadcast on public television during educational programming. Even though the broadcast was for educational purposes, the court believed that it affected the market for the full performance and, therefore, ruled that it was not fair use.

Monster Communications, Inc. v. Turner Broadcasting Systems, Inc. Thirty seconds of footage of a Muhammed Ali boxing match was used in a biographical documentary about the famous boxer. Because this represented only a very small portion of the entire fight and was used for informational purposes, this was ruled to be fair use.

Roy Export Co. Estab. of Vaduz v. Columbia Broadcasting System. One minute and fifteen seconds were used from a 72-minute Charlie Chaplin film for a news report about the death of the comic actor in 1982. Despite its brevity, the court believed the portion taken represented the "heart" of the movie and ruled that it was not a fair use.

Italian Book Corp. v. American Broadcasting Company. A news crew filming a live event inadvertently recorded and broadcast a live band playing copyrighted music in the background. Because the music was not what the reporters were trying to record, only a small portion of the song was broadcast, and there was no evidence the broadcast did any harm to the market for the song. It was ruled to be a fair use.

Campbell v. Acuff-Rose Music. A rap group named 2 Live Crew used the words from the first line of the song "Pretty Woman" in a parody, despite the initial protest of the song's publisher after being approached about the idea. Because only those few words of the song were used, however, it was deemed a fair use.

Dr. Seuss Enterprises v. Penguin Books. Characters from Dr. Seuss books were used to mock the O.J. Simpson trial without permission from the owner of the Dr. Seuss copyright. Deeming the work to be a satire and not a parody, and that it had been done with a commercial purpose, the court ruled it was not a fair use of the Dr. Seuss characters.

Publicity and Privacy Rights

Copyright is not the only area of the law that podcasters might find themselves facing. Another possible issue is publicity rights, or the right of a person to control how his or her voice or picture is used by others, especially if that use could possibly damage his or her reputation. Publicity rights are largely a matter of state law in the United States, but they broadly focus on a few principles. First, the law distinguishes between public and private figures. Public figures are people like celebrities and politicians who are already well known to the general public. Private figures are the rest of us, generally unknown beyond our local communities and our circle of acquaintances. In general, private figures have much broader protection in publicity and privacy rights than public figures. The First Amendment's freedom of the press applies here. You have a right to portray public figures, like politicians and celebrities, in your podcast without permission provided you follow two guidelines. Your representation of them should be truthful, and you cannot make it seem like they are supporting your podcast. For private individuals, the rules are stricter, and you should get in the habit of always getting signed explicit permission from an individual before you use their picture or the audio from an interview in a podcast.

Trademarks

Trademarks are something you might need to be wary of as a podcaster. You should remember from the section on copyright that things like titles, slogans, and names cannot be copyrighted by their owners. That does not provide you with complete liberty to use them, however. They are quite likely to be trademarked. This identifies it as a mark that applies exclusively to their property. Examples of trademarks include company names, logos, and even portions of names used in an entire series. Whenever an individual or a company comes up with a name, logo, or slogan for their products, they will usually register a trademark for it with the United States Patent and Trademark Office (**www.uspto.gov**). Whether they register the trademark or not, they will be entitled to at least some protection of their trademark. Registered trademarks can be identified by an ® symbol, and unregistered trademarks will have a TM symbol.

As a podcaster, there are two ways you could potentially find yourself in violation of a trademark: trademark infringement and trademark dilution. Infringement occurs when you use a trademark in a way that has the potential to confuse your audience about the role the trademark owner has in your podcast. If you name a podcast about tennis shoes *The Nike Show*, after the popular brand of sports clothing and shoes, you will be infringing upon a trademark. The use of the Nike brand would lead listeners of your podcast to believe that you were in someway associated with or sponsored by the sports wear manufacturer. A great deal of your culpability will depend on context. A podcast entitled *The Nike Show* about sports wear is certainly infringing; however, if the show were about Greek mythology and named after the Greek goddess of victory, Nike, the sports company, might not be particularly happy, but they would have a much harder time proving infringement. Listeners are unlikely to reach the conclusion that Nike is involved with your show.

Unfortunately, Nike is such a popular trademark that such a show might still be in hot water. Though not infringing, there are special rules that apply to especially well-known trademarks, like Nike and its famous swoosh mark. These are known as trademark dilution laws, and they seek to preserve the value of trademarks by preventing their overuse, even in non-infringing ways. It can occur one of two ways. First, through trademark blurring, which occurs when a mark is used in other contexts, such as a "Nike Show" about the Greek goddess Nike. It might still have a defense if it could demonstrate that it was a noncommercial show.

Another, more serious, source of dilution is trademark tarnishment. A trademark is tarnished when it is used in a morally offensive way or in association with a product of inferior quality. In short, there is a risk of a tarnishment charge if the owner of a trademark can make a case that the unauthorized use has the potential to damage his or her product's reputation. For example, a pornographic film in which the actor or actress is very visibly wearing clothes with the Nike logo. This is unlikely to give consumers the impression that the company is associated with the pornographic video. The producers might not have even realized the logo was visible during filming. Nike would still have the right to object to its logo being portrayed in a morally offensive context. Of course, this does not apply to legitimate journalism. Although Nike could stop a pornographic film that displayed its logo without permission, a negative product review is considered a protected use.

You are not completely barred from using trademarks in your show. If your use is done in an informational context, is not potentially morally offensive, and does not imply an association between your show and the company that owns the trademark, you should be OK. But just like with fair use, showing good faith can be important in trademark issues. If you use a trademarked logo, name, or slogan during the course of your podcast, and feel confident that your use is not infringement or dilution, it does not hurt to include a disclaimer that clearly distances you from the trademark owner. It will never immunize you from charges of infringement or dilution, but it can go a long way to show that you are at least trying to play by the rules should your use of a trademark inadvertently cross a line one day.

As with copyright, trademark law can be complicated, and both the federal government and the individual states each have their say in precisely what is permitted and forbidden. If you want to use a trademarked work or image in your podcast, you should consult a lawyer first to ensure that you will not be liable for infringement or dilution or find an alternative way to express the idea. The Greek mythology "Nike Show" can probably avoid a lot of trouble and legal fees by going with the name "Mythology Hour."

Choosing a License

After all this talk about the rights of others, you might be wondering if you have any rights at all. All the rules that apply to everyone else also apply to you, which means you get the same protections. One of these is the right to choose which license, or rules, you will provide your podcast under.

All rights reserved

U.S. copyright law defines the maximum protection you receive for your work, and to claim the full scope of it, you can place the phrase "All Rights Reserved" in the copyright tag for your podcast. This gives you exclusive control over the distribution of your individual episodes and how your listeners can use them. The All Rights Reserved model is so restrictive that it may be technically illegal for your listeners to copy your podcast onto their MP3 players. The only limits are those discussed in the sections on fair use and the public domain. Even if you do not place the All Rights Reserved phrase in your podcast, U.S. law will assume that this is the licensing model you are using.

Implied license

No matter which licensing model you choose, you should be aware of the concept of an implied license. With an implied license, you receive the full protection of the All Rights Reserved model, with the exception of any protections that your own actions imply you do not wish to receive. For example, though it is normally a violation of copyright law to download whole copies of copyrighted material, the fact that you will, as a podcaster, be putting the material up yourself and advertising its presence in podcasting directories implies that your listeners have an implied license to download it.

Creative Commons

Though the All Rights Reserved model offers the greatest possible protection, many podcasters feel the license is too restrictive. It seems a bit ridiculous to license a podcast under rules so restrictive that it is borderline illegal to download it onto an iPod. On the other hand, the scope of possible implied licenses is worrying as well. For this reason, artists, podcasters, and other creative professionals banded together to create the "Creative Commons" licensing system. This provides a total of six licenses for podcasters to choose from that are written with the realities of Internet distribution in mind. The six licenses are:

- Creative Commons Attribution
- Creative Commons Attribution Share Alike
- Creative Commons Attribution No Derivatives
- Creative Commons Attribution Non-commercial

- Creative Commons Attribution Non-commercial Share Alike
- Creative Commons Attribution Non-commercial No Derivatives

As you can see, the licenses are grouped according to the podcasters attitudes on four activities that a listener may wish to do with a podcast they have downloaded:

- **Attribution**: All the Creative Commons licenses share this trait. It allows your listeners to make as many copies of your podcast as they wish to make and even give copies to their friends and distribute it themselves. The only condition is that they give you credit whenever they do so.

- **Share Alike**: Share Alike is a special license restriction that says that listeners may make copies and distribute your software as much as they like, but they must use the same license you used when they do so.

- **No Derivatives**: This restriction ensures that your work is not modified by others. To the degree the law allows, it prevents your work from being used in remixes and parodies.

- **Non-commercial**: Finally, this restriction stipulates that others may not use your work for a commercial purpose.

Creative Commons Attribution

This is the most permissive license possible under the Creative Commons framework. It not only allows your listeners to copy and distribute your work to others, but also gives them a free hand to modify it and use it in remixes, parodies, and as part of their own work. It in effect states that the only right you wish to maintain as the work's creator is the right to be given credit. Other than that, the work, essentially, is public domain. Think carefully before choosing this license, because it gives a lot away. Should your work become incredibly popular, it would allow a recording company to package your work on a CD and sell it in stores without ever paying you a penny, so long as they give you credit as the creator.

Creative Commons Attribution Share Alike

This license is only slightly more restrictive than the plain Attribution license. It allows listeners a wide range to do what they like with your work, but it insists that they always do it under the same license. This still leaves commercial activity open to them. A company could take your podcast, package it on a CD, and sell the CD in stores without paying you, provided they gave the CD the same Creative Commons license.

Creative Commons Attribution No Derivatives

With this license, your listeners are free to pass your work around amongst themselves, but they are barred from making any modifications to your podcast. Unless the user has a fair use, the work must be kept whole and unmodified.

Creative Commons Attribution Non-commercial

Under this license, listeners are free to use and pass your work around and even modify it to create derivative works of their own, but they are barred from any commercial gain they might receive in doing so.

Creative Commons Attribution Non-commercial Share Alike

This combines the "Attribution Share Alike" license and the "Attribution Commercial" license. This license permits users to use your podcast in their own derivative works, but insists that those works cannot be used for commercial gain and must be distributed under this same license.

Creative Commons Attribution Non-commercial No Derivatives

This last and most restrictive Creative Commons license combines all the traits. Users may share your podcast among themselves and make any copies they like. However, they must give you credit for your work when they so do, they must not do so in a way that earns them a commercial gain, and they must not use your work as a source in creating others.

What about Fair Use?

U.S. copyright law defines the broadest possible set of protections you can claim for your podcast, which means any use of your podcast that would be considered a fair use under copyright law would also be considered a fair use under the Creative Commons license. For example, if a user decides to create a parody of your work, a la Weird Al Yankovic, and can successfully claim that his or her parody is a fair use, the No Derivatives clause in the Creative Commons license will not protect you. It might, however, make the parodist appear to have acted in bad faith, because you had explicitly stated that you did not want such things done with your recordings.

Public domain

Even with the most permissive of the Creative Commons licenses, you retain ownership over your show; however, nothing prevents you from giving up even that. Should you choose, you can simply declare that your work is part of the public domain that all copyrighted material joins 70 years after the death of its creator. This will make the podcast free in every possible sense of the word. Placing your podcast in the public domain is a drastic step, however. The action is irreversible, and, in the United States, you will surrender all your rights in regard to it. You might even surrender the right to be given credit for the work, depending on the nature of the podcast you created and the state in which you reside.

Chapter 13

Video Podcasting

Most podcasts to date have only an audio portion. Audio is cheaper to make and host and can be recorded while you are wearing only your underwear. However, a growing number of podcasts include video, sometimes even HD video, in their shows. This is often called a vodcast, which combines the words video and podcast. In most respects, video podcasting works the same as audio podcasting. WordPress (with a podcasting plugin), Podbean.com, and other podcasting services will support video using exactly the same steps as required for audio only shows. You will still want a low noise floor and a good microphone. The only differences are in the production itself and in potential hosting. Aside from YouTube, there are very few free video podcasting hosts out there. Even a video podcast with a modest viewership of a thousand people can easily chew through four-hundred gigabytes of bandwidth per month, which can get a little expensive.

Two video podcasting solutions will be covered here: Apple's iMovie, the video equivalent of the GarageBand software used in the audio chapter, and a combination of VideoSpin and VirtualDub for Windows. These tools allow you to capture and edit video as well as add special effects like titles and transitions. In addition, they all allow you to export to a multitude of formats, including automatic uploads to YouTube, if you prefer to distribute your videos using their service. All of this software is used as examples. With the exception of iMovie, which is only free with the purchase of a new Apple computer, they are all free and the lessons learned with these programs will transfer easily to any program you choose to use to create your video podcast.

Apple iMovie

Apple iMovie is a nonlinear video editor. Nonlinear video editors allow you to capture video in a series of clips, which iMovie calls "Events," that are then combined, either in whole or in pieces, in a project. It is called nonlinear, or "not in a line," due to its ability jump instantly to any section of a recording and move it directly into the project. This makes even fairly sophisticated editing tasks as easy as dragging and dropping clips into the sequence the editor wants to appear.

Capturing

As soon as you open iMovie, you will be presented with the choice between creating a project designed to be viewed fullscreen on a standard monitor, an iPhone, or a widescreen monitor. This is known as the aspect ratio, or the width of the video, measured in pixels, compared to the height. For a standard monitor, there will be four pixels (or dots) horizontally for every three pixels vertically. That works out to about 1.3 horizontal pixels for every one vertical pixel. For widescreen, it will be sixteen pixels horizontally for every nine vertical. That is about 1.8 pixels horizontally for every one vertically. The iPhone is about half way between the two: three vertical for every two horizontal, or 1.5 vertical for every one horizontal. Ultimately, the choice is up to you, but widescreen monitors are quickly becoming the new standard, so that would make a good choice.

Click the button that looks like a small camera to activate the video capture. A new window will open using the built-in iSight camera as the capture device by default. You can go with that or, if you have another digital camera, select it from the camera drop down box. You are also given a choice between all the supported resolutions (or video sizes) of that camera, some of which might or might not be in the aspect ratio you selected. Ideally, you should always record in the same aspect ratio as your final project, but if you cannot and need to record in a different aspect ratio than the final project, then it will be automatically cropped — or have the edges cut off — to fit the ratio of the final project. For example, if you record in the standard aspect ratio (4:3), but choose to publish your project as widescreen (16:9), the tops and bottoms of the recorded image will be cut off to make the image fit. Alternatively, if you prefer the solid black bars on the edges familiar to everyone watching widescreen or standard aspect ratio content on a television screen that does not support it, you can choose this by right-clicking your project name, selecting "Project Properties," and choosing "Fit in Frame" under "Initial Video Placement."

Determine Aspect Ratio

When selecting a supported camera resolution, you are not given the aspect ratio and are left to determine it for yourself. Doing this is simple. Either by hand or with a calculator, divide the width (the first number) of the resolution by the height (the second number). For example, one common resolution for non-HD cameras is 640x480. To determine the aspect ration, divide 640 by 480 to receive a result of around 1.3. By dividing the width and height of the standard aspect ratio (4:3), you get the same answer. A standard resolution 640x480 is. On the other hand, 1024x576 divides out to approximately 1.8, the same as the widescreen ratio (16:9).

You should be staring at a preview of exactly what the camera sees and what would be recorded if the capture was turned on. If you are using the built-in iSight camera, you should also see a small green light on your computer. Click "Capture" to begin recording.

You will be asked to choose whether to create a new "event" to hold your recording or store the recording in an existing event. Remember, iMovie stores clips in events, and then the events are combined in bits and pieces to form a project later during post-processing. Choose to create a new event and give it an appropriate name, such as "Marshall Plan Episode Master Copy."

You will also be given a choice of hard drives to save the video to and an estimate of how much video will fit on that drive in terms of minutes. Depending on the video size you have chosen, you should be able to get around fifteen minutes of video per gigabyte of free hard drive space.

As soon as you click "OK," there will be a brief delay of a few seconds and the recording will begin and continue until you click

"Done." Wait until you are absolutely certain that the recording is happening before you begin to speak. While the computer is preparing to record, you will not see the camera's image in the preview updating.

Do not worry if there is some dead time at the beginning and end of the video. This can be easily removed during editing. It is far better to have five or ten seconds of dead time recorded and remove it than to record a new episode from scratch because the first few words were cut off in the beginning. Unlike pure audio podcasts, it can be difficult to seamlessly add second takes to the middle of a recording in video if you were not planning a scene transition at that point anyway.

Once you have finished your show, click "Done."

Importing from a digital camera

You do not have to capture clips live using iMovie. You can also perform your recording using a digital camera and import the data from the camera directly into an event. Simply connect your camera to the USB or Firewire port and choose the option "File" and "Import Movies."

You will be given the chance to select the digital video files directly off the camera and a choice of which event to move the data to. You will also be free to decide whether the video is cleared off the camera as it is imported or left on the camera.

Editing and post-production

When you finish, you will have one or more clips stored in the event library at the bottom of the screen. To move a clip into the project (at the top of the screen), you can use two methods. First, you can click and drag a portion of the clip to move just that area into the project, or you can right-click the clip, choose "Select Entire Clip," and drag that into the project.

When clips are added to the project, they will playback in a seamless fashion, with no pauses between each section. However, the project view will leave a small space between each discrete clip. This is to give you room to add transitions and other special effects.

Adding sound effects and background music

IMovie comes with powerful and easy to use tools for adding sound effects and music to your video podcast. At the right of the screen, there is a panel of four buttons: a musical note, a camera, a "T," and a fade in process. Naturally enough, these stand for "sound effects," "movies," "titles/subtitles," and "transitions." Choose the musical note to open the sound effects.

By default, you are free to add music and sound effects from four sources: the built-in iMovie sound effects, the "iLife" sound effects used in GarageBand, all of your GarageBand projects, and your entire iTunes library.

Go to the iTunes library section and choose a song you like. Drag it into the project and it will appear as a transparent green box. Press spacebar and you can see your video with background music from your iTunes library. Keep in mind, you will need permission from the song's owner to use the song in a distributed podcast, but the ability to use songs from iTunes is available in iMovie.

Now, choose the "iMovie Sound Effects" and find the "Alarm" sound effect. Click and drag the alarm on top of your project. The interface provides two ways you can drop a sound effect into the project. If you drop the sound effect directly on top of the clip, then it will play over (and with) the background music. However, if it is dropped near (but outside) the clip, it will interrupt the music effects. Drop your sound effect directly on top of the clip. You can see where it located because it will appear as an opaque green box beneath the preview of your video. You can move it around by clicking and dragging. It will tell you the length of the sound effect as well: 5.1 seconds. And if you press the spacebar to preview the effect, you will hear that there are a total of eight alarms that will sound. Next, you should edit the effect so that only one alarm will sound.

Now, right-click this opaque, green box and choose "Trim." The project view will be replaced with an audio waveform view that should look familiar if you went through the tutorial on GarageBand, surrounded by two golden bars. Drag the right-most golden bar so that only the wave for the first alarm is between the two bars, and click the play button to test your selection. When you are done, click "Done."

You will be left with a dramatically shortened audio clip, around 0.6 seconds and a single alarm buzz.

If you hit the spacebar now to preview your project, you should have your video with background music and a single alarm buzz somewhere in your project. Just like in an audio podcast, you should usually begin and end your show with a bit of music.

Animate a static photo

If you have an ordinary photograph that you would like to use in your project, there are two ways you can insert it into the video: as a static photo or animated, using the "Ken Burns" effect, made popular by its use in documentaries produced by filmmaker Ken Burns. Click the camera icon. You can import still photos to your project and animate them from either iPhoto or Photobooth. Choose a photo and drag it into your project tree in the location where you would like it to appear. After you have done this, it will appear in your project, and if you move your mouse over it, you will see three icons. Choose the one that looks like a square. This is the "crop" command. There are three options for how you crop your photo that will appear in your preview window: Fit, Crop, and "Ken Burns."

Choose Ken Burns. Two boxes will be overlaid on your photo: a green "Start" box and a red "End" box. Click and drag these boxes so that the green box is smaller and surrounds only the most important area of the photo and the red box is larger and a little off center. Hit the spacebar. The effect will be a slow zoom out and pan from the foreground of the photo to the entire photo. By using this effect, you have some movement to keep the video interesting even during periods when a still photo is used.

Add transitions

Just like with an audio podcast, you can add a bit of professional flare to the show by marking scene changes and the opening and closing of the episode with a transition. Click the button that looks like an hourglass. IMovie comes with a dozen transitions built in. Select "Cross Dissolve," and drag it into your project, placing it in the blank space before the static photo you added in the previous step. This will cause the video to dissolve slowly into the static photo. It will appear as a small hourglass shaped box in the break between the clips. If you move your mouse over it, you can see the duration of the transition, and by right-clicking, you can alter the duration. Drag another "Cross Dissolve" into the space after the photo.

Finally, drag "Fade Through Black" to the very end of the clip to have everything fade to black in the end.

Add opening and closing titles

Simple transitions like "Fade Through Black" can do a lot for the visual appeal of the episode, but you can do better using the titles feature. Click the "T" button to switch to the titles screen. IMovie comes with a dozen built-in title effects, and they cover everything from credit rolls to subtitles. Find the title named "Echoed," and drag it into the beginning of your project. This places the title at the bottom left of the screen in white letters, and echos it in a transparent shadow across the entire bottom third of the video. In the project view, it will appear as a blue bar above the video. Click the blue bar, and you will be able to edit the text of the title. Enter the name of your show, and your name for the title and subtitle.

Now, drag the "Scrolling Credits" to the end of your project, just before the "Fade Through Black" transition. Double-click each credit to edit it to give credit where it due.

Keynote Titles

IMovie provides the basic titles for you, but if you want something a little more stunning and you own a copy of the iWork office suite with Keynote, you can use its "Export" feature to create your own titles screens that can blow away the simple effects available in iMovie. Any project you can create in Keynote can be turned into a movie added to your project, which means you have all the effects and transitions in Keynote at your disposal.

For a fast example, open Keynote and create a new default project. Click the text box on the page, and click the "Inspector" button. Go to the "Build" tab (the flying yellow diamond) and choose "build out." Select effect "flame," and set the duration to three seconds. This will cause your title to burn up in a flame and disappear.

Click File, Export, and "QuickTime." Select "Fixed Timing" as your playback method and choose "Next." Name it "Fire Title." Now, go back to iMovie and choose "File" and "Import Movie." Go to your Movies folder and select "FireTitle." Drag it into your project, and now, you have a cool animated title sequence that will make all your friends jealous.

Publish to YouTube

Now that your project is finished, all that remains is to release it to the world. IMovie makes it easy to publish our videos directly onto YouTube. YouTube gives you only very limited options for branding your video channel page and has fairly strict community guidelines, not to mention a hard limit requiring each video to be no more than ten minutes long. However, it is also the only free quality video podcasting host.

Click "Share" in the main menu and "YouTube." Enter your account name and password and choose between the allowed resolutions. Enter a title and description, and click "Next." The upload will begin automatically.

Publish to disk

Nothing forces you to use YouTube. If you have another hosting service, such as Podbean.com or a WordPress-based host, you can publish videos using the same steps you used to publish audio. To save your video to your hard disk in a format that will be understood by other hosts, select "Share" and "Export Movie." You will again be given a list of supported resolutions and a helpful guide to how well those resolutions will be supported by various devices such as iPods, iPhones, and YouTube. If you move your mouse over the "i" information icon, you will also be given an estimated file size. A minute of video will range between half a megabyte to 20 or 30 megabytes, depending on the options chosen.

VideoSpin and VirtualDub

VirtualDub (**www.virtualdub.com**) is a simple utility for Windows created by the open-source community to capture video from any device plugged into the USB, Firewire, or the video-in port of a computer. It can be downloaded free of charge from the website. If you wish to record directly from an attached webcam or other device, you will need a copy of VirtualDub. However, if you have a digital camera that creates its own computer video files, you can skip VirtualDub and go straight to VideoSpin to import from a digital camera.

VideoSpin is a free editor from Pinnacle Software. After you capture video with VirtualDub, you will use VideoSpin to edit, add special effects, and do some other simple post-production work, such as add titles, transitions, and export directly to YouTube. Should you wish to expand the abilities of VideoSpin, such as adding MP4 support, you can purchase the necessary add ons from Pinnacle Software.

These two programs will be used for the Windows portion of the tutorial. You could also replace these programs with Windows Movie Maker, but it provides only the bare minimum of functionality.

Capturing

This tutorial will be broken up into two main steps: recording (or capturing) and post-production. The capture portion will be done with VirtualDub and post-production and editing with VideoSpin. Download and start up VirtualDub. Unlike most Windows programs, it will not create an option in your start menu by default. Instead, you should extract it to a folder named "VirtualDub" on your Desktop. Within that folder will be a file named "VirtualDub.exe." Double-click that, and you will be on your way.

To enter video capture mode, ensure that your camera is connected to the computer and click "File" and "Capture AVI." The top bar of the screen will change to read, "capture mode," and a preview of the video in your camera will appear immediately on the screen. However, recording is not occurring; this is just a preview. Before you do anything else, you need to specify which file on the hard drive will hold the master copy of your recording. Click "File" and choose "Set capture file..." You might also want to select "File" and "Allocate Disk Space." This ensures that you have some space set aside on the drive that is ready to receive video data, prevents lost frames, and can help compensate if you have a slow hard drive that has not been run through the Windows defragmentation utility in a long time.

Name the file "video_podcast_ep01.avi," and save it to your desktop. Now, you are ready to record. Press F5 (or click "Capture" and "Capture Video") to begin. As soon as you are finished, press Escape (or click "Capture" and "Stop Capture"). There is no need to finish. The data is written out the disk while the capture occurs. Just close VirtualDub, and start up your copy of VideoSpin.

Import from digital camera

Before editing, let's assume you want to import a few clips from a digital camera into VideoSpin to use in this episode. If you do not have a digital camera, feel free to skip this section.

Once VideoSpin is open, select "File" and "Import Media from Device." Choose your device in the source drop box and click the "Import" button. The videos will be placed on your Desktop by default, and the photos in your "My Pictures" folder.

Editing and post-processing

VideoSpin uses a slightly counter-intuitive interface for loading files. Ensure that the "Camera" on the left side of the screen is clicked. This is the media-loading icon. Just to the right of it is the browser. Select a directory from the directory drop down box (your Desktop is chosen by default), and it will give you a list of four files in the directory. Just underneath it are two small blue arrows. Click them to browse through the directory until you find your clip. When you find it, double-click it. VideoSpin will automatically detect scene transitions in the clip (or try to) and separate them into different clips. This process might take anywhere from a few seconds to a few hours depending on the length and complexity of the clips. If you have a particularly long video you are importing and a particularly slow computer, you might want to take this chance to go get a cup of coffee. Once it has finished, the file browser will be replaced with anywhere from one or two to dozens of clips from your video file.

At the bottom of the screen, with the Pinnacle logo emblazoned over it, is the project timeline. It has a total of five tracks: two for the video and its audio, a titles and transitions track, and a track each for sound and background music. Let's add an opening and closing title.

Opening titles

You do not want to open your video directly to camera footage; the first few seconds of your show are your chance to make a good impression, so you should always begin with a title. Click the "T" icon on the left side of the screen and your clip browser will turn into a selection of around 20 built-in titles. They range from the professional to the zany. Choose the one that reads "The Crazy Bunch" in a comic book style font and drag it to the very beginning of the titles track. After it is there, right-click it and choose "Go to Title Editor." Click one of the words and hit the backspace key to delete the entire title and replace them with the name of your podcast. Click OK. You will repeat this when it comes time to do your closing title as well, except you will place the title at the end of the project rather than the beginning.

Transitions

If you click the play button in the top right of the window, you can see that, right now, your first clip will play with the title emblazoned over it for a few seconds at the beginning. Really, your

video should gradually fade in, so click the lightning bolt tab to go to the transitions. There are literally dozens of transitions available, so take some time to browse through them. You can see a description of what each title does by hovering your mouse over it for a few seconds. In addition, if you click the transition once, it will play a short preview. For now, just choose the first one, "Fade in and out." Drag it into your video track and hit the play button. Your title will appear on the screen, and your video will slowly fade in from black behind it. If you would rather have the title fade in with your video, this can be easily done, just drag another copy of the fade into the titles track.

You will also want a transition between clips. To do this, drag another clip into project view and choose the "Dissolve" option this time. This will cause the image of the previous clip to slowly transform into the next clip, so that, in the middle of the transition, both clips are clearly visible on the screen.

Add a sound effect

VideoSpin comes with a small library of sound effects, so click the speaker tab to select one. You will be given a choice of five categories: animals, background, crowds, miscellaneous, squeaks, and vehicles. Choose "Background," and drag the rain clip into the sound effects track of your video. This is the one with a speaker next to it.

Add some background music

Unfortunately, VideoSpin does not come with a selection of royalty free background music for your choice, but it does provide a link into your Windows "My Music" folder. You can select any music from the folder and drag it into the music track of the project. Be careful with this, however. Ensure that you own the rights to use any music in your podcast. Otherwise, you might find yourself in court rather than a recording studio. *See Chapter 12 for more information on copyright law and fair use.*

Publish to disk

Save your work, and it is time to publish to disk so you can upload your video podcast to the world. Look at the top of the screen, and find the "Make Movie" tab. Choose "MPEG-4" under file type and "Full Size (good quality)" under the presets. Click "Create File," and your project will be exported to the disk as a video file that you can upload your to podcasting host. Depending on your computer speed, the length of your movie, and the number of transition and other special effects that you use, this could take anywhere from a few seconds to hours. It will give you an estimate of the total time before you start. If it is long, click "OK," and go get a cup of coffee. Also, this will likely consume all your computer's resources, so before you decide to do anything too strenuous on your computer, bear in mind that it will slow down your movie publication.

Publish to YouTube

Like GarageBand, VideoSpin can also publish directly to YouTube. To do so, choose the "Make Movie" tab and select the "Web" icon. Select "YouTube" and choose create. Bear in mind, YouTube limits its users to no more than ten minutes (and 100 megabytes) per video.

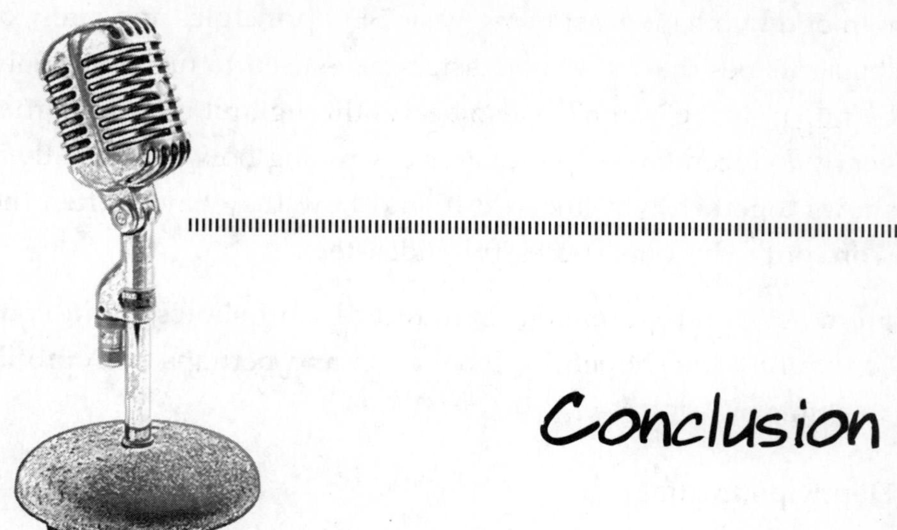

Conclusion

Having finished the book, you should have a solid idea for a podcast, highly targeted at a specific niche using the principle of hyper-specialization, and how to produce the structure that makes a podcast sound professional. You should be familiar with at least one audio recording and editing program, including how to do basic post-production work to get the most out of your recorded audio, and at least one nonlinear video editor and capture utility. You should be able to look at a room with a keen eye for what traits will make it the best studio on a budget, and you should have on-hand experience with at last two possible hosting solutions, along with the technical knowledge you need to make an informed choice when it comes time to choose a hosting service. And though I sincerely hope you will never need it, you should even have a grasp of the legal issues that can confront a poorly informed podcast creator. Finally, you have learned how to market your podcast using basic SEO principles and a few of the strategies that other podcasters have used to turn their hobby into a career. You have also heard, throughout the book, from nearly a dozen fellow podcasters discussing how they put their shows together, why they do it, and how they have gotten the word out to become successful podcasters.

From here, all that remains is to record your shows, build your community, and hopefully, have a fun and perhaps even profitable time of it.

Happy podcasting!

Appendix A

RSS Tags

The RSS format is the heart of how podcasting works. It provides a simple language that can be easily read by both human readers and computers. Ideally, you will always use an automated solution to work with your RSS feed, but if something goes wrong, you might need to roll up your sleeves and dive into the RSS code yourself. The following guide covers all the tags that make up the RSS format as it applies to podcasts.

<copyright>: This holds your copyright notice. It is not necessary because your podcast enjoys full copyright protection within the United States even if you do not use it. However, if you wish to use a more precise license, such as the Creative Commons license, you must say so here. Example: <copyright>Copyright 2010 All Rights Reserved</copyright>.

<description>: This is a short description of your podcast within the <channel> section and a short description of your episode within each <item> section. ITunes does not recognize this tag and, instead, requires that you use the <itunes:summary> tag. Example: <description>This show will cover a number of important topics.</description>.

<enclosure>: This is a complex tag that provides the podcatcher with the information it needs to find and download each episode of the podcast. At minimum, it provides a link to a podcast episode, the length of the episode in bytes, and a special code for the type of data the podcast file uses. Example: <enclosure>url="http://podcast.com/episode003.mp3" length="2321432"type="audio/mpeg"</enclosure>.

<guid>: Every <item> (episode) in your podcast must have this tag, and the contents must be unique within your podcast. If it is left out, or if two episodes have the same <guid> tag, then podcatchers will not be able to download the podcast properly. Most podcasters handle this by making the <guid> equal to the URL for each episode. Example: <guid>www.mypodcast.com/episode110.mp3</guid>.

<image>: This gives the podcatcher the information it needs to associate an image with your podcast. It is a fairly complicated tag to use. ITunes does not recognize this tag; you must use the <itunes:image> tag along with it. Example: <image><url>http://www.mypodcast.com/albumArt.jpg</url><height>100</height><width>100</width></image>.

<item>: Within your podcast, the <item> tag will hold each episode. This is a nested tag that will hold many other tags. At the minimum, it must have a <title>, <description>, <guid>, and <enclosure> tag within it to work. Example: <item><title>Iron Man Versus Freddy Krueger</title><link>http://www.mypodcast.

com/Episode-103IronManVsFreddy.MP3" length="10298132" type="audio/mpeg"/></item>.

<itunes:author>: This gives credit to the author of the podcast. It might or might not be the same as the <itunes:owner> tag. Example: <itunes:author>Kevin Walker</itunes:author>.

<itunes:explicit>: This marks podcasts or episodes that have mature content so the iTunes podcatcher can prevent children from accessing them. Foul language and sexual innuendo require this an explicit tag. Pornographic content, on the other hand, is banned outright from the iTunes podcast directory. Example: <itunes:explicit>yes</itunes:explicit>.

<itunes:image>: This tag, rather than the <image> tag, is used to attach an image to a podcast that will appear in the iTunes podcatcher. Example: <itunes:image> http://www.mypodcast.com/episodeart.jpg</itunes:image>.

<itunes:keywords>: This allows you to specify 12 keywords that describe your podcast to help the iTunes search engine direct interested listeners to your show. Abuse of the tag is also grounds for banishment from the iTunes podcast directory. Example: <itunes:keywords>New England birdwatching birds Maine Vermont birdwatcher Jersey York Connecticut</itunes:keywords>.

<itunes:owner>: This is used to give credit to the owner of the podcast. It can be the same as the <itunes:author> tag or different. Example: <itunes:owner>Kevin Walker</itunes:owner>.

<itunes:subtitle>: This is used to provide a very short description for your podcast, usually only one or two sentences in length. Example: <itunes:subtitle>A great podcast</itunes:subtitle>.

<itunes:summary>: This is used to provide a short description for your podcast. It is similar to the <description> tag used by most other podcatcher software. Example: <itunes:summary>The cloud show is a weekly podcast about all the great ways clouds affect our lives and our culture, hosted by Charles McLoward.</itunes:summary>.

<language>: This describes the language the podcast's content is in. Most likely, you want to set this value to "en-us" for U.S. English. Example: <language>en-us</language>.

<link>: This contains a URL, or a website address, such as www.mypodcast.com. In your podcast's RSS feed, it should be used within the <channel> section to provide a link to your podcast's website and within the <item> section to provide a link to the media file holding your podcast episode. Even though this provides a link to the episode itself, this is not what the podcatcher will use to find the podcast episode. Most podcatchers, including iTunes, use the <enclosure> tag for that. Example: <link>www.mypodcast.com</link>.

<pubdate>: This is optional inside your podcast's RSS feed that holds the date that the podcast was produced. It must be formatted according to precise rules. Example: <pubdate>Thu, 12 Jun 2010 14:00:00 CST</pubdate>.

<rss>: This is an essential part of every podcast's RSS feed. It should one of the first tags in the RSS file, and its closing tag (</rss>) should be the last. It tells the podcatcher software that the podcast feed is using the RSS format. *You can see an example of a complete feed, with RSS rag, at the beginning of Chapter 8.*

<title>: This describes the title of the podcast or an individual episode in a podcast's RSS feed. Example: <title>My podcast</title>.

Appendix B

Useful Services for Your Podcast

You might find the following services helpful when you are starting your podcast. They range from hosting services to affiliate programs and advertising networks.

Blubrry: Blubrry is a podcast host powered by the powerful WordPress CMS and their own open-source podcasting extension. They do not have a free version of their hosting service, but they do have a free ad and affiliate network that can be joined by anyone with a podcast.

Podbean.com: Podbean.com is a podcasting hosting service with multiple tiers of service, starting at free of charge and increasing in price from there. It builds the RSS feed for you and give you your own fully integrated website, blog, and podcast in one location.

WordPress: WordPress is a popular content management system (CMS) designed for blogs, but podcasting is supported using the "PodPress" plugin. A variety of Web hosts support WordPress sites. WordPress itself is free, and it even offers two gigabytes of free space for bloggers and podcasters. For an audio-only podcast, this is generally enough space for over 30 hours of content.

YouTube: For video podcasts on a budget, it is hard to beat the online video giant YouTube. Users can register for free and immediately begin uploading as many videos as they want to a massive community. Individual videos are automatically part of Google search results under the "Video" link. Many video podcasting tools like Apple's iMovie support automatic uploads to YouTube when the work is finished. It is not without its flaw however.

Finally, some producers who discuss controversial topics have found themselves running afoul of YouTube's community nature. YouTube enforces its guidelines using a "flag" based system where users can click a link to flag an episode, or an entire show, as objectionable. This causes it to be temporarily removed until it can to be reviewed by moderators. Most false flags are overruled by the moderators and the videos return to the service quickly, but organized groups of objectors can still keep a service down by routinely and constantly flagging videos. Hackers have even written "flagbots," which are computer programs that automate the process of flagging videos as quickly as a targeted user can put them up. For most producers, this is not a problem, but those who prefer to talk about topics that might be the subject to passionate disagreements might prefer to pull out their credit cards and pay for a hosting service rather than allow their content to be held hostage.

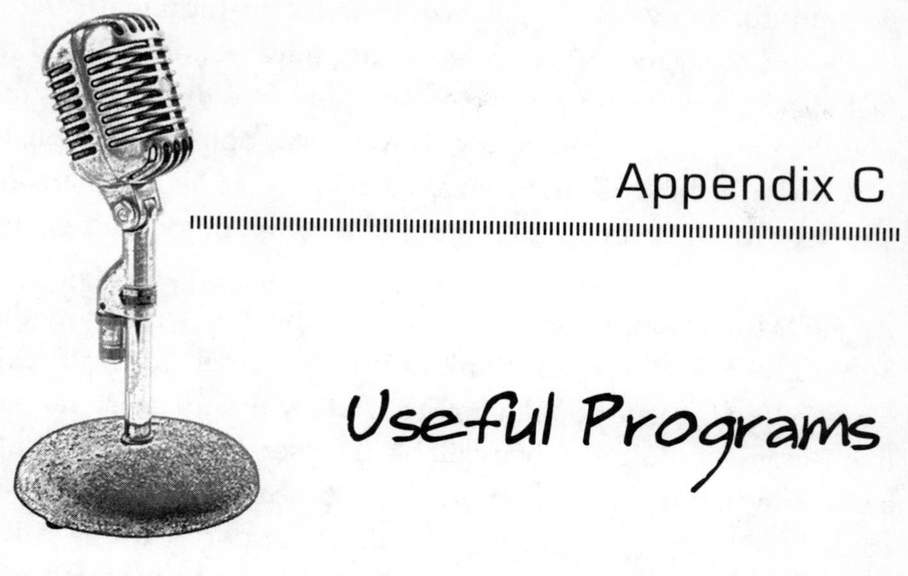

Appendix C

Useful Programs

You might find one or more of these programs useful while building your podcast.

Apache: Apache is one of the most important programs on the Internet. It is this program that powers most websites, including those that hold podcasts. It is also, like Audacity, completely free to use, but has a substantial learning curve to use effectively. Most podcasters will want to go with one of the existing hosting services, but if you feel that self-hosting is the way to go, Apache will be an essential tool in your arsenal.

Apple GarageBand: Apple GarageBand is a part of the iLife suite of media applications that come with most new Mac computers and can be bought separately for approximately $100. It streamlines the process of recording, editing, and completing other post-production work on podcast episodes, including attaching logos and other metadata professional podcasts are expected to include. It comes with a variety of royalty-free music loops for fading in and out of your show, as well as a sophisticated music sequencer that allows you to create your own jingles using an on-screen or MIDI keyboard. It is a popular program for podcasters.

Apple iMovie: Apple iMovie is a part of the iLife suite of media applications, and you can think of it as the video equivalent of GarageBand. It is a popular program for video podcasters, but like GarageBand, it is only available for users of Apple computers. It can import video from most digital camera models or record directly from any USB webcam. It supports adding titles and subtitles, as well as common video effects such as wipes and fades.

Apple iTunes: Apple iTunes is the most popular podcatcher on the Internet, due to its easy-to-use integration with Apple's iPod music players and the iTunes podcast directory. More than any other individual podcatcher, as a producer, you should make it a priority to ensure that all aspects of your podcast works as expected with this program. A dedicated podcast host will usually support iTunes by default, with no extra effort on your part, but if you take a more difficult route, you might need to take the iTunes tags upon yourself.

Audacity: Audacity is a recording, editing, and post-production program created by the open-source community. It is free and runs on every major operating system, including Windows, Mac OS X, and Linux. It is not as easy to use as some commercial programs, nor does it include bells and whistles like GarageBand's built in MIDI sequencer. Rather, it is designed around the open-source GNU philosophy of "Do one thing and do it well." It contains everything needed to record, mix, and produce podcast episodes and is capable of working with other software to include jingles and theme music.

Cyberduck: Cyberduck is a client for Mac OS X computers. Smart FTP is a related program for Windows users. If you elect to work with an existing hosting service, they will almost certainly give you two options for how to upload your files: a Web interface and an FTP account. The Web interface is easy to use, but they are usually limiting and even a little unreliable for large files like videos and audio. Cyberduck allows you to upload files directly to your hosting service without depending on Web forms and can even automatically restart and resume downloads to ensure that interruptions in service do not interfere with your upload and waste your time.

Appendix D

GarageBand Sound Enhancements

The following sound enhancements and special effects are part of the GarageBand program. Some will be more useful than others, depending on the type of show you create. Many are designed with musicians, rather than podcasters, in mind:

Amp simulation: The guitar and bass amp simulators mimic the effect of an amp for electric guitars and basses. This allows musicians to plug their instruments directly into the computer for a recording.

Auto wah: Auto Wah simulates the effect of a "wah wah" effect pedal for electric guitars and pianos. It is also known as an "envelope filter." It is called a "wah" because it alters the sound of the incoming music to produce that sound.

Automatic filter: The automatic filter is a complex effect used when creating music using GarageBand's synthesizer. It muffles and raises the volume of a track alternately according to a regular pattern every few seconds. It is useful in creating techno-style music, but less so in other sound effects.

Bitcrusher: The bitcrusher is used to dramatically reduce the bit rate, or the quality, of a portion of audio. Like the automatic filter, it is commonly used in the production of techno music, but it can also be used as a special effect on vocals to produce a robot like voice.

Chorus: Chorus takes a single input sound and modifies it to produce the sense that the sound is coming from more than one source. For example, a single speaker can sound like an entire crowd of people speaking in unison.

Compressor: The compression compressor adjusts the volume of the loud and quiet portions of the recording to reduce the difference between them.

Distortion: Distortion is an effect meant for people using GarageBand as an amp for their electric guitars. Depending on how much is used, it can range from making a guitar sound "warmer" to the noisy, gritty sound of some heavy meatl bands.

Echo: Echo does exactly what it sounds like – all sounds are echoed. The higher the setting, the more dramatic the echo. However, even at its low settings, this is intended to be a special effect more than an enhancement. If a given section of your podcast should suggest that you are speaking from a canyon or a cavern, this is appropriate.

Flanger: The flanger is a musical effect that duplicates the audio recording and plays both the original and the duplicate, with the duplicate delayed slightly. The timing of the delay is changed slowly over the course of the effect. This produces a very slight echo that causes the pitch to rise and fall slowly. An example of this effect is the Beatles song "Tomorrow Never Knows."

Gate: The gate watches the volume level of the audio coming into the microphone and only records the sound when the volume exceeds a predefined level. However, it does not remove ambient noise from the recording — only from the silent portions. Think of the gate as a switch that automatically turns the microphone on and off when it is needed. Used carefully, it can add a bit of depth to the silence of pauses during the show, but over-used it can be distracting.

Overdrive: An effect intended for guitarists. The sound is driven beyond the dynamic range of the recording deliberately to produce the resulting distortion as a musical effect. Unless you intend to produce a podcast that features your own electric guitar music, it is probably not of much use to a podcaster.

Phaser: A musical effect similar to the Flanger, but without the delay effect. It can be a difficult effect to describe, but you can hear an example at the following site: **http://en.wikipedia.org/wiki/Flanging**.

Reverb: Reverb is like a gentle echo. Whereas as echo produces a sound that resembles what you get if you shout at the Grand Canyon, reverb, even at its highest settings, produces an effect more similar to speaking in a hallway. Unlike the echo, a subtle use of reverb can enhance the quality of a podcast. A complete lack of reverb can give the impression that the speaker is a disembodied voice, while a little reverb mimics the effects of sound bouncing off walls in a real environment.

Speech enhancer: The speech enhancer plugin combines a number of other plugins, including a noise reduction filter, in one interface and set of presets.

Track echo: This is a more detailed version of the echo effect that allows for a finer control over the traits of the echo, including delay time and volume of the echo.

Track reverb: This is a more detailed version of the default reverb control. Rather than simply setting the amount of reverb, you can set the delay time, the percentage of sound that will be used in the reverb, and how long it lasts.

Treble reduction: The treble reduction enhancement allows you to specify a frequency ceiling, and GarageBand will dampen sounds above the frequency.

Tremolo: Tremolo is a fancy term for the effect produced by an electric guitar's "whammy" bar. It produces a trembling effect in the recording. It is intended primarily for musicians.

Visual EQ: The Visual EQ allows you to adjust the relative volume of different frequencies in a recording. By doing this, you can emphasize one set of the spectrum while reducing another. GarageBand comes with dozens of presets, including things like "Add Bass Clarity" and "Add Presence to Thin Sounds." This is more useful in podcasts with a musical focus to emphasize the lower or higher pitched aspects of music.

Vocal transformer: The vocal transformer enhancement is a set of presets that attempt to modify the pitch of a recorded voice. Presets include things like "Male to Female," "Female to Male," and "Chipmunk."

Appendix E

Audacity Sound Enhancements and Special Effects

The following effects and enhancements are available as part of the Audacity program. Some can be very complex compared to others, and many are designed with musicians – rather than podcasters – in mind.

Generated Effects

Audacity provides the following tools for creating your own sound effects from scratch. Many of these effects are intended primarily with techno-musicians in mind, but here is a fast run down of what they do, should you think one of them might be suitable for your show.

Chirp: This effect produces a quickly rising tone similar to the sound effects of a 1980s video game.

Click track: The click track represents a built-in metronome. This effect produces a track that contains nothing but simple beeps in time.

DTMF tones: This effect produces the phone dial tones for a given set of numbers.

Noise: This effect produces static noise.

Pluck: This effect produces a realistic-sounding guitar pluck. It allows you to specify the pitch (using the MIDI code) and the duration.

Silence: This effect produces a segment of total silence.

Risset drum: This effect produces realistic drum sounds.

Tone: This effect allows you to specify a frequency and produces that steady tone for as long as you like.

Enhancements

Audacity provides the following enhancements for altering the sound of your podcast. Many of these will be better suited to your podcast.

Amplify: This enhancement allows you to specify the number of decibels to increase the volume of a track.

Bass boost: This enhancement increases the volume of only the lowest pitches in the recording.

Change pitch: This enhancement raises or lowers the pitch of the entire recording. This can be used to produce "chipmunk" voices or other similar effects.

Change speed: This enhancement allows you to speed up or slow down the track and alter the pitch accordingly. This is similar to the effect of playing a vinyl record on the wrong speed setting. Speeding up the track will increase the pitch, and slowing it down will decrease the pitch.

Change tempo: This enhancement allows you to speed up or slow down the track without altering the pitch.

Click removal: This enhancement allows you to remove clicks and pops. This can work as a cheap replacement for a pop filter.

Compressor: This enhancement compresses the range between the highest and lowest volumes into a narrower range.

Cross fade in: The cross fade in enhancement will fade in the selected track at the same time as it fades out the other tracks.

Cross fade out: The cross fade out enhancement fades out the selected track while fading in the others.

Delay: This enhancement is similar to an echo effect, but there is a "bounce" in the echo.

Echo: This enhancement adds echos to the sound.

Equalization: This enhancement allows you to adjust the sound using a visual equalizer.

Fade in: With this enhancement, all tracks are slowly faded in from silence. This is a good way to begin the show.

Fade out: With this enhancement, all tracks are slowly faded out from silence. This is a good way to end the show.

Hard limiter: The compressor causes high volumes to be reduced slowly and gradually, so that rises in volume are still perceptible, but they are not as dramatic as they normally would be if uncompressed. The hard limiter places an absolute maximum limit on volume.

High pass filter: With t his enhancement, lower frequencies are de-emphasized in favor of higher frequencies.

Leveller: This enhancement forces dramatic changes in volume to occur more slowly and gradually.

Low pass filter: With this enhancement, higher frequencies are de-emphasized in favor of lower frequencies.

Noise removal: This enhancement takes a sample of noise and attempts to remove it from the entire recording. This can be a very powerful effect.

Nyquist prompt: This sophisticated command allows audio programmers to specify a series of text commands for Audacity's sound enhancement tools.

Phaser: This is a musical effect similar to the flanger, but it does not have the delay effect. *See "flange"in Appendix D.*

Repeat: Repeat the selected area of the recording a number of times regularly throughout the track. For example, if you use the risset drum effect to generate a drum stroke, you can use repeat to have this repeat over the course of the entire recording every second.

Reverse: If you ever wanted to make your own experiment in backmasking, this is your tool. The material you record will be reversed and played backward in the final recording.

Sliding time scale/pitch shift: With this enhancement, you can adjust both the speed and pitch of the recording.

Tremolo: This is a fancy term for the effect produced by an electric guitar's "whammy" bar. This enhancement produces a trembling effect in the recording.

Truncate silence: Witht this enhancment you can strip all silent portions beyond a certain length from the recording.

Vocal remover: This enhancement attempts to strip the vocals from a recording, while leaving nonvocal elements untouched.

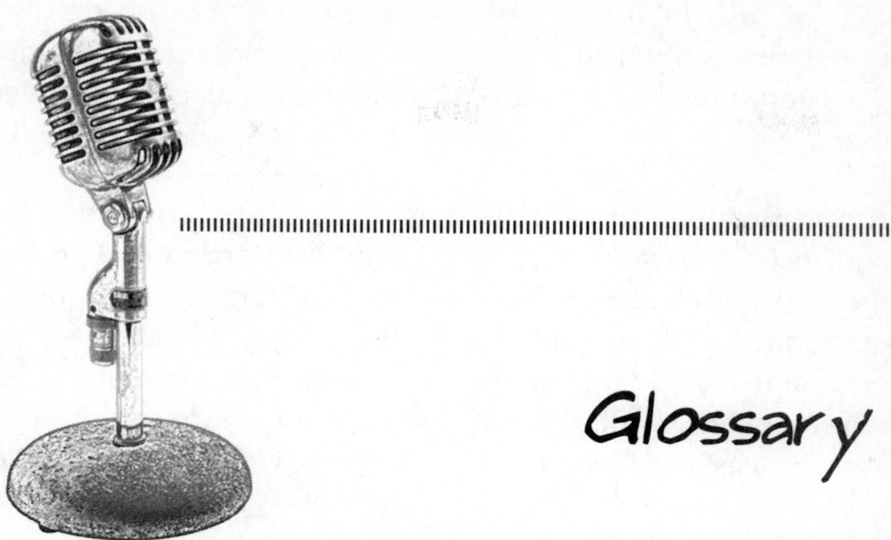

Glossary

Acoustics: The science that studies the way sound travels and interacts with different materials.

Ad network: Rather than interact with advertisers directly, podcasters can subscribe to an ad network. These services use keywords and other techniques to connect podcasters and advertisers indirectly. They make it easy to get started with advertising immediately, but generally, they pay far less than other advertising arrangements.

Advanced Audio Coding (AAC): The successor of the classic MP3 format. It is generally superior, delivering higher quality and consuming less disk space, but it is not as widely supported as MP3s.

Affiliate program: An advertising method in which the podcaster earns a commission on any sales that can be traced back to their program. Usually, upon joining an affiliate program, the podcaster gets a dedicated URL he or she can use to direct users to the product, which allows the sales to be traced back to them.

Ambient noise: Undesirable and distracting sounds from the surrounding environment, such as those made by pets and home appliances, which can be recorded during your podcast production.

Apache: The most popular Web server software used on the Internet today. It is free and open source and is sponsored by a collection of companies and academics known as the Apache Foundation. *See open source.*

Aspect ratio: The ratio between the width and height of a video image. Common resolutions include 4:3, the standard resolution used by older monitors and televisions, 16:9, the widescreen resolution used by most new HDTVs, and 16:10, which is used by many computer monitors.

Audacity: An open-source audio recording and editing program that can be downloaded and used freely on any computer.

Audio Interchange File Format (AIFF): A lossless format for storing audio. It is not suitable for distribution, but it is a good format for master copies. It is the Apple equivalent of Microsoft and IBM's WAV format.

Backlinking: This refers to the number of links leading to a website from elsewhere on the Web. They are an important aspect of SEO strategies. *See SEO.*

Bandwidth: This can measure two things: the total amount of information that can be communicated over a network before having to pay extra fees or the speed that the information can be communicated over the network. It is usually measured in terms of megabytes or gigabytes. Available bandwidth will be a major component in your choice of a hosting service for your podcast.

Bit rate: A value used to describe the quality of recorded audio or video. It is expressed in either kilobits per second (kbps) or megabits per second (mbps). It measures how much information is stored for each second of a recording. MP3 typically uses a bit rate between 32 and 312 kbps. The meaning of the bit rate changes for each audio format; 256 kbps for an MP3 is generally considered equal to 1411 kbps for an audio CD.

Bit: The smallest measurement of computer disc space. A bit corresponds to a single one or zero in binary code. Internet speeds and the bit rates that measure the quality of an audio or video file are usually measured in terms of bits per second.

Black hat SEO: A technique that refers to dishonest or unscrupulous SEO methods. Generally, this involves tricking the search engine into believing either that a website or podcast is more popular than it is or that it contains information it does not really contain. *See white hat SEO*.

Blog: Short for Web log. A blog is the Internet equivalent of a regular newspaper column. Both blogs and podcasts can use the RSS feed as a driving technology.

Byte: A measurement of computer disc space. A byte contains eight bits. It is roughly the size of a single letter in a plain text document. File sizes usually use bytes as their measurement, and download speeds are usually expressed as bytes per second.

Cardioid microphone: A microphone pick-up pattern. Cardioid microphones pick up sound in a heart shape area around it, with most sound coming from the front, but some muted sound being allowed in from the rear and sides.

Client: The opposite of a server. The client is a machine or a program that asks for and receives information from a server. Examples of clients include podcatchers like iTunes and Web browsers like Internet Explorer.

Closing tag: The RSS feeds that provide the table of contents for a podcast are made up of a series of opening and closing tags that contain the information for the podcast. The closing tag always comes last and always looks identical to the opening tag, except with a forward slash added. For example, the opening tag <tag> corresponds to the closing tag </tag>. *See opening tag.*

Cloud computing: A technology that allows multiple computers, networked together, to work together in such a way that they appear to be only a single computer. This allows a Web service, like a podcast, to consume and pay for only the computer resources it needs while having a nearly unlimited supply of computer power available to draw from when needed. Examples are the Amazon Cloud and the Google App Engine.

Codec: A computer program designed to translate information into and out of an audio or video format. For example, to convert the sound from a microphone into an MP3 file, an MP3 codec is required. All programs discussed in this book come with their own MP3 codec.

Compressor: A device or software program that reduces the dynamic range of an audio signal and, therefore, reduces the difference between loud and soft portions.

Condenser microphone: A microphone design in which sound is converted to electricity through the motion of two charged metal plates. They tend to be more expensive, but to produce a fuller, more accurate sound compared to dynamic microphones, but they are also much more easily damaged.

Copyright law: Laws that protect a creator's right to control how his or her work is used.

Cost per thousand (CPM): The "M" stands for "mille," the Latin word for thousand. Some advertisers pay podcasters and other Internet media sources based on a CPM method, where the podcaster earns a set fee for every 1,000 viewers.

Crop: To resize an image or video by chopping off corners or edges, usually done in order to convert an image from one aspect ratio to another.

Dead air: A broadcasting term for unnaturally long periods of silence during a recording. It should be removed in the post-production phase.

Decibel (dB): A measurement of sound volume.

Dedicated hosting: A hosting service that assures the customer the full resources of a physical computer. This is usually overkill, even for highly successful podcasts.

Diaphragm: The part of a microphone that is vibrated by incoming sound waves. Though the method used varies with each type of microphone, it is the vibration of the diaphragm that is translated into recorded sound.

Domain name system (DNS): The Internet technology that translates URL Web addresses (like **www.google.com**) to numerical IP addresses that can be understood by a computer. *See URL.*

Domain name: The major part of a URL that identifies a computer on the Internet. For example, in the URL **www.google.com**, the domain name is google.com.

Downstream bandwidth: The total speed an Internet service provider makes available to its customers for receiving information over the Internet. It is the most prominently advertised Internet speed because most residential Internet users download more content than they upload. *See upstream bandwidth.*

Dynamic IP: A method ISPs use to assign IP addresses to their customers in which the IP address assigned to each computer changes regularly. This allows more computers to share a smaller number of addresses, but it also makes it more difficult for podcasters to use their own computers as a server.

Dynamic microphone: A microphone design in which sound is converted to electricity through the vibration of a magnet. These microphones tend to be cheaper, but more rugged, than condenser microphones.

Dynamic range: The dynamic range of a recording is the difference between the loudest and the quietest parts of the recording. It can also refer to the range of volume that a microphone can successfully capture without distortion.

Evergreen content: Podcasting and Web content that never goes out of date. This SEO principle states that content that stays relevant for a long period of time is likely to draw more traffic over the long run than content that is valid or of interest only for a very short time.

Extensible Markup Language (XML): The computer language used in an RSS feed to power podcasts.

Fair use: The legal concept that allows a person to copy material that is under copyright without getting permission from the copyright owner for a limited range of uses. It exists to give critics, reporters, and researchers some peace of mind when publishing small, insignificant excerpts in the course of their work. The boundaries of it can be subtle, however, and you should always consult with a lawyer before deciding that a given use is fair.

Feedback: A sound anomaly that is produced when a microphone attempts to record its own sound coming through a speaker. It sounds like a high-pitched squeal.

Feed verifier: A program or website that checks a podcast's RSS feed to ensure that it conforms to standards and will work correctly with podcatchers.

Flattr: A social networking site that makes it easy for fans to make small donations to websites, blogs, and podcasts they like or want to support. Each member of Flattr contributes a set amount per month that he or she wishes to donate, and the amount is distributed between each episode the user "flatters" by clicking a link on the website.

Frequency response: The frequency response describes how accurately a microphone responds to different frequencies. A perfect microphone would have a flat frequency response, recording all frequencies evenly. However, in reality, all microphones will tend to have difficulty with the deepest sounds and tend to exaggerate high-pitched sounds to some degree.

GarageBand: An audio recording and editing program developed by Apple to allow users of the Mac OS X computers to publish podcasts. It comes free with most new Apple computers.

Gigabyte (GB): A shorthand term that refers to 1024 megabytes. It is usually used to measure the size of particularly large files or hard discs. A standard DVD is 4.7 GB in size.

Gigahertz (GHz): A measure of processor speed that means "a billion times per second" and measures the times per second a computer can perform a programming instruction. Modern personal computers usually have one or two processors running at 1.5 to 3 gigahertz.

H.264: A video format designed to reduce the size of a video so it can be transmitted over the Internet and stored with a minimum loss of quality. It is used by YouTube, iTunes, and Blu-ray movies. It is part of the MPEG 4 family of formats.

Hyper-localization: A form of narrowcasting in which a podcaster targets his or her podcast primarily at the residents of a local area, such as Texas or Chicago.

Hyper-specialization: A narrowcasting strategy in which a podcaster targets his or her podcast specifically at a narrow area of interest.

Implied license: In copyright law, a license that is implied by the actions of the copyright holder. For example, the right of a user to make copies of a podcast episode onto their own computer, which is normally illegal under copyright law, is granted by an implied license by the podcaster publisher who hosts the podcasts on his or her public website.

Intro: Any regular music, phrase, or other event that you use to mark the beginning of an episode. This improves the quality and professionalism of a podcast. *See outro.*

Internet protocol (IP) address: A special number that represents a computer's address on the Internet that allows other computers to find it.

Joint stereo: A technique for saving space when storing stereo audio data. Instead of storing two completely separate audio channels for the left and right speakers, joint stereo stores only one audio channel along with a "side track" that provides enough information to deduce the content of the other track from the first. FM radio uses joint stereo.

Ken Burns effect: An effect used to animate still photos by simultaneously panning and scanning across the photo. Named after filmmaker Ken Burns.

Key frame: A term used in performing lossy compression on video. Rather than store every frame of a video, a single frame is stored every few seconds and the other frames are reconstructed based on that one frame.

Keywords: A selection of words attached to a website that allows search engines to quickly determine the important topics on a website. Proper and efficient use of keywords is an important part of SEO strategy. *See SEO.*

Kilobit (kb): A measurement 1024 bits. It might be used to measure the bit rate of an MP3 file or the speed of a slow Internet connection. A short sentence written in Notepad can be approximately a kilobit in size.

Kilobyte (kB): A measurement of 1024 bytes. It is usually used to measure the size of small files on a computer or download speeds. A medium-length paragraph written in Notepad can be approximately a kilobyte in size.

License: The agreement between a podcaster and his or her listeners over the rights and responsibilities of each.

Lossy compression: Computer techniques that reduce the file size of audio and video content by throwing away information in a way that the audience is unlikely to notice. This is generally successful, as shown by the success of lossy formats like MP3 audio files and MPEG-4 movies, but multiple uses of lossy compression can lead to dramatic decreases in quality.

Machinima: A type of parody or satire popular among young podcasters. It uses the art and engines of 3D video games to create stories that mock the video games they are taken from.

Media kit: A two- or three-page brochure about your show and its advertising options that can be distributed to potential advertisers.

Megabit (Mb): A measurement of 1024 kilobits. It can be used to measure the bit rate of a video file or the speed of a fast Internet connection.

Megabyte (MB): A measurement of 1024 kilobytes. It is usually used to measure the size of a file or a small hard drive. A standard CD is 700 MB in size.

Megahertz (MHz): A measure of processor speed. It means "million times per second," and tells you how many times per second the computer can perform a programming command. Modern computers usually have one or two processors running at 1500 to 3000 megahertz (or 1.5 to three gigahertz).

Metadata: Literally means "self data." Information embedded into an audio or video file that describes the content of that file. Your podcast episodes should include metadata, such as the title and artist, both in the RSS feed and within the audio or video file itself.

MIME type: A special code used to describe different file types. For example, MP3 files are described by the MIME code audio/mpeg.

Mixer/mixing board: A device that combines audio from multiple inputs into one signal. Built into the mixer are controls for adjusting the relative volume and stereo placement of each source of sound, such as multiple microphones or a CD player for background music. A mixer can be extremely important for podcasts that need multiple microphones live at any one time, but it is not really needed for podcasts using only one live mic because most of

the functions provided by it can be done in software.

Moral rights: A legal right of a creator to receive credit for his or her work and spare it from distortions. Recognition of moral rights changes a great deal from country to country. Creators tend to keep moral rights, even if they have sold or lost the copyright.

Moving Picture Experts Group (MPEG): An industry association responsible for issuing technology standards for the movie industry. Examples of standards published by MPEG include the popular MP3 audio format and the MPEG-4 video formats.

MP3: A popular lossy audio format. It reduces the size of audio files by discarding sounds that most listeners are unlikely to notice. The proper name is MPEG-1 Audio Layer 3.

MPEG-4: A family of video and audio formats designed for use on computers and the Internet. They include the H.264 video format, the M4A audio format, and a variety of others.

Musical Instrument Digital Interface (MIDI): A protocol for storing musical notation for computer playback using digital instruments. MIDI can be produced directly on a computer or on an electronic keyboard.

Narrowcasting: A marketing strategy that targets a relatively small portion of a large population. It is opposed to broadcasting, which targets a large number of people within a relatively smaller population. Narrowcasting is an important part of choosing a podcasting subject because it can dramatically reduce the number of podcasts competing for your listeners.

Nested: A structure can be divided into individual sections that contain other sections. Podcast RSS files use this structure. For a podcast, there will be a <channel> tag that describes the podcast and contains multiple <item> tags that describe the individual episodes.

Networking: The practice of building and cultivating mutually beneficial relationships with others in your field.

Noise floor: The ambient noise picked up by the microphone even when the host of the podcast is completely silent. One of the challenges of budget recording is finding cheap ways to reach the lowest possible noise floor. *See ambient noise.*

Noise-reduction headphones: These contain a special circuit that attempts to strip static, pops, and other annoying noises from the sounds the listener wants to hear. Good for enjoying music, but bad for the podcaster. He or she uses the headphones as a tool during recordings to listen for sources of noise and, ideally, to do something to reduce the noise.

Nonlinear editing: A computerized editing technology that allows a film editor to pull clips from any location in footage and easily reassemble them in any order. IMovie and VideoSpin, used in this book for video podcast editing, are both nonlinear editor, as are most computerized editing programs.

Ogg Vorbis: An open-source audio format similar to MP3. It was developed due to the complex patent situation of MP3, but some MP3 players do not support the format.

Omnidirectional microphone: A microphone pick-up pattern that records sounds from all directions.

Opening tag: The RSS feeds that provide the table of contents for a podcast are made up a series of opening and closing tags that contain the information for the podcast. The opening tag always comes first and always looks like this: <tag>. *See closing tag.*

Outro: Any regular music, phrase, or other event that you use to mark the end of an episode. This improves the quality and professionalism of a podcast. *See intro.*

PageRank: A method used by Google to track the reliability and authority of the pages it indexes. As a general rule, pages with a high PageRank are always shown above those with a low PageRank in the search results.

Parody: A work created to mock another created work. In the context of U.S. copyright law, a parody copies from the material it is intended to mock. It is more likely to be viewed as a fair use than satire.

Pay per click (PPC): An advertising method in which the advertiser only pays for users that follow the advertised link. Google's AdWords program uses this method of advertising.

Peak: The highest volume point reached during a recording.

Pick-up pattern: The way a given microphone type will emphasize or de-emphasize sounds coming from different directions.

Pixel: A single colored dot on a computer or television display.

Plosives: Sounds, such as the "P" in "stop" and the "B" in "bear," which are created by pushing air through closed lips. These sounds have a tendency to make an exaggerated "popping" sound when picked up by a microphone. *See pop filter.*

Podcast directory: A website or online service that maintains a searchable database of podcasts. Examples are the iTunes Store and Podcast Alley.

Podcasting: A method of distributing episodic audio or video content automatically to the audience using Web syndication technology.

Podcatcher: An application on a listener's computer that automatically checks for new episodes of a podcast, downloads them, and moves them to an MP3 player. One of the most popular podcatchers is iTunes.

Podfading: A tendency of smaller podcasts to start, gain a significant audience, and slowly die as the creator loses the motivation to continue with regular releases of content.

Pop filter: A device used to prevent an exaggerated "pop" sound caused when a person uses a plosive sound, such as "P," in front of a microphone. *See plosive.*

Ports: The numbered channels that can be used to communicate with a computer over the Internet. They do not correspond to any physical device; they are simply numbers that allow servers and clients to understand what sort of traffic is being communicated. For example, "80" is traditionally the port associated with World Wide Web (WWW) content like websites and podcasts.

Processor: The part of the computer that performs mathematical operations and controls the rest of the computer.

Promo: A short advertisement, usually between 15 and 60 seconds long, about your podcast that can be exchanged with other podcasters as a way to market yourself. This is similar to a commercial on television or radio. *See quickcast.*

Proximity effect: The tendency of a microphone to lower the pitch of a voice as the speaker gets closer to the microphone.

Public domain: Works that, either at the express wish of their creator or due to age, no longer enjoy any form of

copyright protection. In the United States, works generally enter the public domain 70 years after the death of their creator or 90 years after their creation if they were created by a business.

Publicity rights: The right of a person, especially a celebrity, to control how his or her likeness and voice are used in other creative works.

Quick-cast: A short example of your show that you can exchange with fellow podcasters in your subject. Similar to a guest appearance on a radio or television show. *See promo.*

Random access memory (RAM): A component of a computer that stores information for running programs. Insufficient RAM can be a cause of sluggishness when editing audio in post-production.

Ramble and edit: A recording that is done completely without script and is cleaned up in post-production later.

Really simple syndication (RSS) feed: A text file, written in the computer language XML, which tells a computer where to find the episodes to a given podcast on the Internet.

Resolution: The dimensions of a computer or television display or a video image in terms of pixels, given as widthxheight. *See pixel and aspect ratio.*

Reverb: A sound effect that sounds like a very slight echo. If done with moderation and subtlety, it can improve the quality of the vocals in a podcast, but too much can make a podcast sound like it was recorded in a cave. It can come both from the environment during recording and be added later by a computer or other special equipment.

RSS tags: Commands in the RSS feed for a podcast that are surrounded by arrow brackets (< >) and usually refer to things like titles and descriptions.

Sample rate: One value used to describe the quality of recorded sound. It is expressed in kilohertz (kHz) and is a measurement of the number of times in one second an audio file stores information in a recording, but not the amount of information stored. Audio CDs use a sample rate of 44 kHz.

Satire: A created work intended to mock another work or aspect of society in general. In the context of U.S. copyright law, a satire copies material from one work in order to mock something completely different.

Self-hosting: Instead of hiring out a service to host a podcast, the podcaster uses his or her own computer for the task. This can save a great deal on hosting fees, but it requires a fair amount of technical know how.

Search engine optimization (SEO): A marketing strategy that studies how to use keywords, back linking, and other techniques to improve a site's rankings in search results. There are both legitimate and disreputable ways to implement SEO strategies.

Server: Either software that sends, or serves, Web and podcast content to a recipient or the client, or the computer that runs that software.

Server farm: A facility that holds hundreds or thousands of networked computers in one place and leases their use out to podcasters, webmasters, and others. Large Internet companies, like Google, can have their own dedicated server farms.

Shared hosting: A hosting service in which a podcast shares a server with other websites and podcasts. Quality of service varies a great deal depending on the price. There are shared hosting services dedicated to podcasters that offer a variety of services not offered by generic shared hosts, the most important of which are automatic RSS feed

generation and updating and automatic addition to the major podcast directories.

Signature: A feature on many social media sites, such as Web forums, in which users select a short amount of HTML code to be attached to everything they post. It can be used to promote your podcast without being perceived as spam by most webmasters and visitors.

Social media: A term that describes websites like Facebook and Twitter that are designed to build and foster communities of people.

Sound card: A hardware device built into most computers that handles both incoming and outgoing sound. A dedicated podcaster might wish to invest in a more sophisticated sound card, but it is not an essential tool.

Spam: A slang word used to refer to unsolicited advertisements sent over the Internet.

Speech recognition engine: A computer program that analyzes a recording of spoken conversation and translates it to raw text.

Static IP: An IP address that is assured by the ISP to change only in very rare circumstances. Static IPs make it much easier to self-host your podcast, but usually cost more than a standard residential Internet service.

Sub-domain: The minor part of a URL that identifies a specific segment of a domain name on the Internet. It might be on the same computer or a different computer from the one identified by the domain name. For example, in the URL **www.google.com**, the subdomain is "www." Though "www" is the most common subdomain for domains that have only one website, it is common for hosting services to offer subdomains to their clients. For example, a podcast entitled "Happy Podcast" hosted by the Podbean.com service might have the

URL http://happypodcast.podbean.com.

Talking points: A method of scripting a podcast in which, rather than writing a complete script for the show, the podcaster just writes down vague ideas, or talking points, for the ideas he or she wants to express and the themes to discuss over the course of an episode.

Terabyte (TB): A measurement 1024 gigabytes. It is usually used to measure the size of particularly large hard drives.

Trademark: A name, slogan, or image that a company can register with the government to ensure that no other company can use it. There are two broad ways to violate trademark laws: trademark dilution and trademark infringement.

Trademark blurring: A form of trademark dilution in which a trademark loses its value through overuse in other contexts.

Trademark dilution: An act that reduces the value of a trademark without technically infringing upon it. Unlike infringement protection, which all trademarks enjoy, only trademarks that are already well known are entitled to protection from dilution. See trademark blurring and trademark tarnishment.

Trademark infringement: Violation of a trademark by using it in such a way that your audience is likely to be confused about your relationship with the trademark owner. Never use a trademark in such a way that it gives listeners the impression your podcast is sponsored or supported by a company or individual when it is not.

Trademark tarnishment: A form of trademark dilution that occurs when a trademark is used in a way that could harm the owner's reputation, such as in a morally offensive context or in association with products of inferior quality.

Transmission loss: The tendency of a sound to lose volume as it changes from one substance to another, such as from a wall to air.

Unidirectional: A microphone pick-up pattern that only records sound coming from the front.

Uniform Resource Locator (URL): Also sometimes called a Uniform Resource Identifier (URI) or simply a Web address. An example of a URL is **www.google.com**. It is a short string of text that tells a computer how to find another computer over the Internet. *See DNS.*

Upstream bandwidth: The total speed an ISP makes available to its customers for sending information out over the Internet. If a podcaster chooses to self-host, this is the most important measure of bandwidth. It is usually not clearly advertised and is nearly always less than the downstream bandwidth, which is more prominently advertised. *See downstream bandwidth.*

Variable bit rate: A technology that automatically changes the bit rate as needed during a recording to save space during times when there are only simple sounds and increases quality when needed to represent more complex sounds.

Virtual host: A hosting scheme that strikes a compromise between the control offered by a dedicated host and the affordability of a shared host. Each service runs within its own virtual machine that is given the illusion of having exclusive control of a single computer, while actually sharing a physical computer with a variety of other services. *See virtual machine.*

Virtual machine: A recent technology that allows a computer to hold numerous imaginary, or virtual, computers, each with its own operating system, installed applications, and settings. This technology makes the virtual hosting scheme possible. *See virtual host.*

WAV: A lossless audio format that stores audio data with no attempt made to compress the size of the information. A typical CD-quality WAV file can require as much as ten megabytes of storage space per minute of audio.

Waveform: A graphical depiction of a recorded sound that displays the sound as a rising and falling wave. Loud areas appear as larger waves, while quieter areas appear as smaller ones. This is a useful tool when editing a podcast in post-production.

Web ring: A website that collects a ring of websites related to a topic. In order to be part of the ring, each website is expected to add a banner ad for the Web ring to its own page with a link that allows the user to proceed to the next website in the ring.

White hat SEO: Used to refer to standard SEO methods that attempt to drive traffic to a website or podcast without employing dishonest methods.

Windows Media Audio (WMA): The native format for the Windows Media Player. It has both lossy and lossless versions, but it is not well supported outside the Windows operating system.

Bibliography

Cangialosi, Greg and Irelan, Ryan and Bourquin, Tim and Colette, Vogele, *The Business Podcasting Book: Launching, Marketing, and Measuring Your Podcast*, Focal Press, Burlington, MA, 2008

Geoghegan, Michael and Klass, Dan, Podcast Solutions: The Complete Guide to Audio and Video Podcasting, Apress, New York, NY, 2007

Harrington, Richard and Weiser, Mark, *Producing Video Podcasts: A Guide for Media Professionals*, Focal Press, Burlington, MA, 2008

Holtz, Shel and Hobson, Neville, *How to Do Everything with Podcasting*, McGraw Hill, New York, NY, 2007

Kent, Peter, Search Engine Optimization for Dummies: A Reference for the Rest of Us!, Wiley Publishing, Hoboken, NJ, 2004

Mack, Steve and Ratcliffe, Mitch, *Podcasting Bible,* Wiley Publishing, Indianapolis, IN, 2007

Morris, Tee and Terra, Evo, and Williams, Ryan, *Expert Podcasting Practice for Dummies: A Reference for the Rest of Us!,* Wiley Publishing, Hoboken, NJ, 2008

Author Biography

Kevin Walker writes computer tutorials when he is not recording one of his two podcasts: the audio-only *ChesterCast* and the video podcast Cranky Young Catholic. He lives in Arlington, Texas, with his wife and their many pets. He records his podcasts from his home office on an iMac.

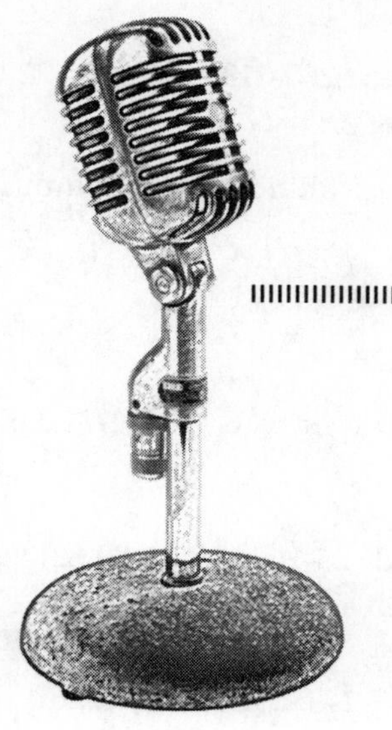

Index

C

D

E

F

G

H

I

J

K

L

M

N

O

P

Q

R

S

T

U

V

W

X

Y